Bury the Corpse of Colonialism

The publisher and the University of California Press Foundation gratefully acknowledge the generous support of the Peter Booth Wiley Endowment Fund in History.

Bury the Corpse of Colonialism

The Revolutionary Feminist Conference of 1949

Elisabeth B. Armstrong

UNIVERSITY OF CALIFORNIA PRESS

University of California Press
Oakland, California

© 2023 by Elisabeth B. Armstrong

Library of Congress Cataloging-in-Publication Data

Names: Armstrong, Elisabeth, 1967- author.
Title: Bury the corpse of colonialism : the revolutionary feminist conference of 1949 / Elisabeth B. Armstrong.
Description: Oakland, California : University of California Press, [2023] | Includes bibliographical references and index.
Identifiers: LCCN 2022030113 (print) | LCCN 2022030114 (ebook) | ISBN 9780520390904 (cloth) | ISBN 9780520390911 (paperback) | ISBN 9780520390935 (ebook)
Subjects: LCSH: Asian Women's Conference (1949 : Beijing, China) | Anti-imperialist movements—20th century.
Classification: LCC JC359 .A67 2023 (print) | LCC JC359 (ebook) | DDC 325/.32—dc23/eng/20220922
LC record available at https://lccn.loc.gov/2022030113
LC ebook record available at https://lccn.loc.gov/2022030114

32 31 30 29 28 27 26 25 24 23
10 9 8 7 6 5 4 3 2 1

CONTENTS

List of Illustrations vii

Introduction
1

1. The 1949 Asian Women's Conference in Beijing (People's Republic of China)
17

2. The Journey to the Conference
59

3. An Anatomy of Revolutionary Women's Praxis
84

4. To Save the World
114

Conclusion
146

Acknowledgments 153
Notes 159
Sources and Further Reading 177
Index 191

ILLUSTRATIONS

1. Asian Women's Conference, Beijing, December 1949 *7*
2. Lu Cui and Marie-Claude Vaillant-Couturier, World Peace Council, Berlin, February 1951 *35*
3. Lillah Soesilo (Suripno), Amsterdam, August 1943 *68*
4. Ho Thi Minh and Jeannette Vermeersch, Asian Women's Conference, Beijing, December 1949 *95*
5. Cai Chang and Marie-Claude Vaillant-Couturier, Asian Women's Conference, Bejing, December 1949 *105*
6. Gita Bandyopadhyay and Betty Millard with Marie Jeusse, Juliette Dubois, Genevieve Denis, and Germaine Huby-Gosselin, in Weissensee, outside Berlin, May 1951 *133*
7. Pak Chŏng-ae, Asian Women's Conference, Beijing, December 1949 *137*
8. Gita Bandyopadhyay and Subash Mukhyopadhyay, West Bengal, undated *144*

Introduction

CELESTINE (MACOUCOU) OUEZZIN COULIBALY

It wasn't as if she was afraid of crowds. Celestine Ouezzin Coulibaly, familiarly known as Macoucou, had spoken to mixed gatherings far from home all her adult life. She knocked on the doors of people she'd never met before, in neighborhoods that didn't know her or her family. She was lucky. She grew up with the knowledge she could lead, maybe even should lead when necessary. Her father led the Sindou canton in Upper Volta. She had an education, a good one, and grew fluent in the French of schooling, great books, and well-honed essays. She traveled the region. She worked as a schoolteacher. By 1949, when she addressed the Asian Women's Conference in Beijing, she was a storied organizer of anti-imperialist women. In 1949, she led the movement of the thousands of women who stormed the prison of Grand Bassam holding over two thousand men from her political party, the African Democratic Assembly (RDA). "The men did not believe in the need for this movement and doubted our ability," she said at the founding conference of the women's organization of the RDA on November 6, 1949.[1]

Her attendance at the Asian Women's Conference might seem surprising, since it was led by and held for Asian women. But the conference was anti-imperialist, and fostered solidarity with other movements against colonial occupation. It was not simply a gathering for women from one colonized continent: it welcomed anti-imperialist women from around the world. Coulibaly's words nurtured the seeds of the African and Asian women's solidarity movement that emerged from this early conference hosted by the Women's International Democratic Federation (WIDF) and the All-China Democratic Women's Federation. Well before the Bandung conference in 1955, the Asian Women's Conference developed an inside/outside political praxis for women's anti-imperialism. The 1949 Asian Women's Conference consolidated a militant, two-part strategy for women's internationalism in the fight against fascism. On the outside of imperial centers, women joined the military resistance against colonial occupation. On the inside of imperialist ruling nations, women fought a war that refused to accept their nations' belligerence abroad. In both locations of struggle, in occupied and occupying countries, this strategy relied upon reaching large numbers of women from rural locales, alongside cities and towns, to join the movement.

Thus, the conference resolutions in 1949 drafted two parts to this strategy, one for women from colonized (and recently independent) countries, and one for women from imperialist nations. In Asia, Africa, and parts of Latin America and the Caribbean, women fought imperialism and feudalism with renewed unity. To do so, they should organize "the masses of women, help to educate them and defend their basic rights!"[2] For women in imperialist countries, their activism should be rooted in an ethical and personal refusal to be accomplices in murder: "Do not permit our sons to kill each other! Stop colonial wars! Insist that your governments recall the troops from Vietnam, Indonesia, Malaya, Korea."[3] This linked strategy mobilized rather than ignored or universalized the differences in women's activism around the world. Internationalist women shared commitments to anti-fascism, anti-white supremacy and anti-colonialism; but their conditions of struggle were specific. This strategy dispensed with allies in the struggle to create accomplices in the fight against fascism, racism, colonialism, and patriarchy. Solidarity was not an invocation of shared intent, empathy or ethics; it was a battle cry enacted.

Conference organizers from the Women's International Democratic Federation invited women from around the world who shared their politics and organizing strategies to build the largest possible women's movement. The popular classes of women, agricultural workers and farmers, as well as wage workers in the informal sectors of towns and cities, joined together to fight colonial occupation. On the inside of colonial powers, women sought to grind the war machine to a halt by refusing to allow family members to enlist, or permit ships to load armaments and soldiers bound for counterinsurgency warfare in the colonies. On the outside of imperial centers, women took up arms, built fortifications, passed intelligence, hid insurgents, doctored the wounded, harvested the crops and fed the frontlines, all to strengthen the fight against occupation. Together they sought to bury colonialism.

Celestine Ouezzin Coulibaly joined this gathering at a critical moment for her own liberation struggle from French occupation. Daniel Ouezzin Coulibaly, her husband, was a leader of his political party the African Democratic Assembly (RDA), and they agreed that enough was enough. When she moved south of her home, she moved to the political center, not of Upper Volta, but one of several centers of Western Africa: that is, the enforced-French-speaking territories of Western Africa. There were other centers, other cities that hosted important meetings for their movement, like Abidjan, like Bamako, like Conakry, like Dakar. The fluid coalition of their political formation both recognized French colonial borders and marked those borders as arbitrary. They questioned the fiction of even "natural" borders: sometimes a river border is more about the river than about the differences between peoples on each side of that river. Worse were the borders that a cartographer drew in negotiation with other imperial mapmakers. The straight lines underscored their own understanding of that territory as a theft not from the land's inhabitants, but from another European tyrant. These borders dismissed the questions that mattered: Where did languages border each other? Where were there distinct cultural practices with an old, yet ever-changing syncretism of overlapping traditions? These maps that named Upper Volta or Ivory Coast as sharply distinct heralded the lines of independence before the people who lived there had decided if they agreed. To build a movement of many locations, often with vast acreages that held very specific histories and antagonisms, was also a necessary fiction. It allowed another set of borders to emerge, or at least, it held a place for a more integral ordering of space. But how easy it was for an anti-colonial independence movement to become a nationalist one: not easy in practice (of building common terms of polity, language, and history) but easy in rhetoric, easy to invoke as a goal standing in for freedom and self-determination.

Coulibaly honored that promise of borders not yet known, of invaders not yet ready to leave but already being shown the exit. When she moved south to the coastal cities of Ivory Coast from Upper Volta, she didn't stay at the level of invocation. Hers was not, strictly speaking, a nation-building project. It was a movement for power taken by the people. When she moved to Abidjan, she went to the markets. That's where the women were. In these markets, French essay-writing was not her most powerful tool. Her voice, alongside her willingness to listen to all that the market women knew and told her, enabled her gift for shaping a collective force that already existed into a political one. Anti-colonialism meant that market women had to listen to rural women: the products of subsistence farming done almost exclusively by women were an integral part of what market women sold. If the collective within the market sphere could extend, consciously, to include the rural lives of women, then anti-colonialism had a network, a supply chain that could break the rough, dangerously aged bones of colonial wealth extraction. It could end the arbitrary and exorbitant taxation demanded so that even the smallest peasant landholder needed cash; the enforced, unpaid labor for the colonizers that ripped children, women, and men from their own grueling work to survive; the practice of filling the most verdant land with crops grown strictly because they would be purchased with European-backed cash. And it could destroy the most devastating of all these policies, the export of these mass-produced food crops far from the people who grew them, far from the people who deserved their nutrients and calories.

In Western Africa, each locality remained a locality. Of course it did. The roads and train tracks so efficient for carting away the bounty often had little to do with the roads and paths traveled for commerce and trade, let alone the extended visits for generational ceremonies of celebration and burial. Colonialism sought replicability: of wealth extraction, of systems of control, of enforced obedience to unilateral demands. Resistance movements sought the power of their masses: of land, of people, of languages, of cultures and creativity. Their movement sought national independence against the borders themselves, borders that were not simply arbitrary, but also violent, since they tore histories, languages, cultures and families apart with a line in a cartographer's notebook. Coulibaly knew the larger strategy of her movement's anti-colonialism. She stayed firmly in the masses and networks of her place, but sought to inspire them to the larger purpose of throwing the occupiers out.

So, when she flew to Beijing, the new capital of the People's Republic of China, in 1949, it is hard to imagine her frightened. That brittle, wintry place welcomed her. Many women from her movement wanted to go in her stead. She was chosen to represent all of them, not just the ten thousand women organized in greater Abidjan, but hundreds of local groups that refused the same colonial occupation, the same colonial robbery. It is easier to imagine how she drew on her family's heritage, on the dignity of her upbringing, on knowing the value of her place. She packed her clothing, not the French-codified uniforms of her schoolgirl youth, but the West African fabrics from her organizing among market women, among farming women, among women of the towns. She wrapped her head using the full intricacy of folds to signify the importance of the occasion as well as her own importance. She probably guessed (here colonialism taught its lessons to her advantage) that she would have to single-handedly make her dress legible in all of its significations: independence of history, willingness to lead, the wealth of her past traditions, knowledge, and its visionary possibilities for the future.

Figure 1. "A Place Where We Think About Humanity" Hall, Asian Women's Conference, Beijing, December 1949. Photo courtesy of Sophia Smith Archives, Smith College.

When she stood up in front of hundreds of people, in the bitter cold of the People's Great Hall in China, with steaming breath and chafed hands, she used French to speak of what they shared. She reminded the delegates of how they had all lived under the boot that sought to scrape away their value, but not because of any inferiority. Quite the opposite. European colonizers bullied their way into unjust overlord status because that value—which they sought to steal—was so rich, because that value could line their pockets. "I am an African woman. I bring greetings from the black women of Ivory Coast, and at the same time I bring their fears, hatred, their living conditions.... Although we are of different origins, different languages, we suffer similarly. And we have the same sense of righteousness."[4]

This is a story about women like Celestine (Macoucou) Ouezzin Coulibaly. This is a story about a theory of anti-colonialism and internationalism that women built. This is a story about a strategy to build socialism, a strategy with women at its center, not on its peripheries. This is a story about one conference held by Asian women in concert with the pro-socialist women of the Women's International Democratic Federation that dared to imagine an African, Asian, Caribbean, and Latin American future without imperialism of any kind. This is a story about one conference held by revolutionary women in 1949 that rippled outward to challenge warmongering as the only way of life. This anti-imperialist internationalism sought peace, democracy and women's rights. Peace included the willingness to fight for a just peace; democracy sought power to the people over monopolies and the aristocracy; women's rights sought the rights to live one's full humanity.

The Asian Women's Conference was held over one week in December 1949. It consolidated an anti-imperialist women's movement, one embedded in the communist and leftist traditions of organizing and Marxist-Leninist theory. Its praxis was hard-won by Asian and African women who organized agricultural workers and farmers, as well as women working in the informal economy for piece rates and minimal wages. This was a mass movement of women rooted in the countryside rather than one fanning out from metropolitan centers. The Asian Women's Conference sought a stage and a megaphone for anti-colonial leaders of communist parties and leftist formations in Asia, but also Africa, the Caribbean and Latin America—yet its traces have been covered over in the archives and our shared political memory on the Left.[5] This story reconstructs an event that enacted as truth global leadership by anti-colonial women working to shape a better future in the ashes of Empire's two world wars. For the legacy of our own present, it recovers the genealogy for feminist internationalism as a praxis, a theory of women's organizing against imperialism.

ARCHIVES, MEMORIES, AND PROPAGANDA

In her diary about the Asian Women's Conference, Betty Millard, a communist party member from the United States, jotted notes about the film shot during the seven days of the conference. On December 17, 1949, she described a "chilly film taken to replace those burned up. Will falsify history considerably—will convey impression the Presidium listened to speakers which was seldom the case. Will also seem the very gay conference since we found our own histrionics amusing...."[6] Two films were created about the conference: one by the Chinese and one by the Russians. However, the footage taken over the six days of the conference burned. The day after the conference ended, it was hastily re-shot. Gita Bandyopadhyay, a key organizer of the conference from the Paris-based central office of the Women's International Democratic Federation, provided a more lighthearted assessment of the two films. In a letter to Millard, she described watching the Russian version in Budapest, Hungary almost a year after the conference. "Yesterday I went to a movie to find you in various moods—mostly laughing. It was the Soviet version of the Asian Women's Conference.... [O]n the whole it was better than the Chinese version and the particular attraction was the Iranian and Indian delegates shouting "Van Sui" which I recognized very much."[7] The celluloid recording the conference burned before the conference ended. Its reconstruction was immediate and on-site, but it was a reconstruction of the event. These records were made by Chinese and Russian filmmakers to portray what happened and who was there. In this educational sense, they are propaganda films that sought to inform and inspire their audiences. Neither film is easily accessible, through digitization or even by mention in the film archives of the former Soviet Union or in China.

In my research, this story began with a conundrum. Until 1951, WIDF records showed that the conference happened, but it was rarely mentioned in WIDF bulletins or pamphlets after this date. Additionally, the usual archives that held substantial records about communist women's movements had no records about the content of the AWC. Memoirs, pamphlets, newspaper articles, and diaries held in these archives described the conference, but none held the official conference documents themselves: the record of discussion among delegates, of participant reports or, most importantly to me, the resolutions or appeals. In part, the lacunae stemmed from the lack of propaganda about the conference. The WIDF never published a transcript of the conference discussions and reports, as it did for its 1945 founding conference, the 1948 Second Congress of Women, and the 1953 Third Congress of Women. Neither did WIDF publish a descriptive brochure to widely share an overview of what happened, as they did for the Mothers Conference held in Lausanne in 1955. The records of the AWC turned out to be hiding, perhaps in plain sight, in the Swedish Labor Movement Archives in Huddinge, Sweden, where the collection was aptly named after the WIDF-affiliated national organization, "The Left Federation of Swedish Women." The conference delegates' speeches were published in the *Information Bulletin*, proof that they were disseminated among members of the WIDF. Even more intriguing, then, is why even the rich holdings of other WIDF materials in the Atria Institute on

Gender Equality and Women's History, the Sophia Smith archives at Smith College, and the International Institute of Social History did not hold copies of the newsletter in their collections from this period. In the Huddinge archives, records of each day's events were carefully typed on WIDF letterhead. They were probably sent to Andrea Andreen, an important executive council member and later vice-president of WIDF who didn't attend the AWC in person. While her personal archives are held in Stockholm, these official records of the AWC proceedings, resolutions, and *Bulletins* were considered organizational records and thus stored in the Huddinge archive.

The absence of records about the AWC outcomes in more well-known archival records of WIDF have shaped how I read these resolutions. Their very hiddenness became a methodological question about "propaganda," since these ongoing decisions of not sharing the conference discussions, appeals and resolutions shaped their meaning.[8] Conference resolutions are often the most public aspect of political meetings like the AWC. In this case, they were the most obscure. Marion Ramelson, the delegate from Great Britain, did not mention any of the appeals or resolutions in her book about the conference.[9] Neither did Betty Millard in her *Daily Worker* articles, nor in her book that described the speeches from the conference.[10] The 1949 AWC resolutions, appeals, and discussions were *not* disseminated widely—that is, they did not become propaganda, or information put in the hands of as many women as possible. This omission of information is particularly strange since delegates at the Asian Women's Conference, and members of the WIDF as a whole, sought to shape a women's movement that spanned the world.

Instead, the political theories for women's internationalist activism developed at the AWC were communicated to audiences in a couple of different shorthands. One invoked motherhood and peace as the alternatives to the unending acquisitive wars of Empire. The language of what I call revolutionary motherhood invoked women as the reproducers not only of people, but of the cultural fabric at large and its ethical commitments to peace. Revolutionary motherhood, in these appeals, sought a global peace that would keep sons and husbands out of the war machine. When these men were conscripted by an imperialist state, revolutionary motherhood intervened to blockade the loading of trains and ships with the materials for war. The other shorthand for women's anti-imperialism in WIDF's public broadsheets appealed more generally to women's solidarity against colonialism as an unjust system, rather than detailing the strategic logic of differential solidarity necessitated by imperialism. Revolutionary motherhood against war and women's solidarity against colonial oppression were the public face for the inside/outside political praxis solidified at the AWC. However, AWC resolutions and appeals were actively hidden by lead organizers, most of whom were members of communist parties. Why weren't these public declarations to anti-imperialist women spread by the WIDF information network among their members? Why were the conference appeals against colonialism, and their theories for a better feminist internationalist praxis, hidden even decades after the conference?

In 1949, anti-colonial, pro-socialist women gave collective voice to a method of global organizing that demanded accountability from all women of the world. That praxis did not entirely disappear for at least two decades, if not longer, since it demanded women's accountability for colonialism and imperialism in global women's movement settings. Yet its explicit address—to women from colonized countries, women of imperialist countries, and sometimes also women from state-socialist countries—was largely absent in the WIDF's own widely-disseminated literature after the Asian Women's Conference ended, with the exception of a Special Issue about the conference and one additional issue of their newsletter, *Information Bulletin*. As a strategy, it defined WIDF's approach to women's anticolonialism, one that fought for peace and explained how peace could require military struggles against violent enemies of nations' right to self-determination. As propaganda, it was largely erased from the public record. The loss of materials and centralized archives for this conference suggests that the erasure of a differential strategy to organize women of the world against imperialism was an active choice rather than an oversight. Instead, for public consumption the WIDF's own publications chose a different mode of address, as seen in the glossy magazine, *Women of the Whole World*, that in 1951 replaced the more rough and ready reports in the *Information Bulletin*.

During the 1950s, WIDF's publications emphasized women's political subjectivity through revolutionary maternalism and their rights to economic and political independence. For public consumption, they supported another kind of unity, a simpler one that invoked political unity among women as mothers and workers and citizens striving for a peaceful world. The Asian Women's Conference strategy was a differential one that addressed women where they stood in order to better address the contradictions of imperialism. Women from colonizing countries had a different activist role than women from occupied countries. But they worked towards common goals: peace, women's rights, and an end to imperialism. Perhaps the blunt tools of propaganda were not up to the task, and the easier unity based on women's common social roles alongside shared political aspirations would have to do. However, the years after the 1949 conference suggest another story, one that's a little more complicated, about how the WIDF's praxis took wings. The traces of this praxis may be hard to find in the archives, but they galvanized a sweeping range of struggles for radical women's activism in the 1950s, particularly visible during the global campaign against war crimes perpetrated by the United States forces during the Korean War.

By the next international WIDF conference, held in Copenhagen in 1953, WIDF had grown tremendously. In five years, over sixty-six countries from around the world had joined the organization. Yet, somehow, the story of the Asian Women's Conference disappeared from the WIDF's own record of its activism, and as a result, from the archives. Archives are regularly culled for the story they tell. Archives are a kind of propaganda in that they advocate in favor of a particular argument by the records they hold, and, as Anjali Arondekar persuasively argues, by what is left out.[11] Archives are never innocent. As propaganda, the archives' silence says something like this: "The 1949 AWC is not an important conference. The AWC did not accomplish anything of record. Look elsewhere. Look at the 1948 Budapest conference; look at the 1953 Copenhagen conference to understand the thinking within the WIDF at this time." Yet the mobilization of the anti-imperialist strategies developed at the AWC powerfully shaped the campaign against the Korean War that began in June, 1950, from the "save our sons" campaigns to the WIDF delegation's brave fact-finding report, *We Accuse* first requested by the Korean Democratic Women's League. The two-part strategy that took women's differential relationship to imperialism and the importance given to leadership by women from colonized countries drew on the AWC's lessons. They shaped the campaign against the Korean War for its three years (1950–1953), as well as other WIDF campaigns in this decade, including their support for the Mau Mau movement for Kenyan independence and their fight against the brutal pass laws that cemented formal apartheid in South Africa.

Left feminism, particularly a communist left feminism for the Third World, currently has no archive, no finding aid. Pivotal actors like Cai Chang of the PRC who joined the Communist Party of China in 1923, Gita Bandyopadhyay of India who had fought against colonialism since she was thirteen, Gisele Rabesahala of Madagascar, who co-founded the communist Congress Party of Independence of Madagascar in 1948, and Celestine Ouezzin Coulibaly, are almost unknown internationally. To delve into the archives of India, Morocco, Algeria, or Lebanon gives more detail of these national anticolonial women's movements. However, all of these archival collections are structured through an active resistance to telling this story of Marxist feminism through anticolonial internationalism. Solidarity among colonized women produced this anti-imperialist internationalism. And its theory depended upon the shared lessons of organizing rural women who fought patriarchy embedded in the feudal-colonial-capitalist relations that oppressed them. These archival occlusions are instances of anti-communism, where leftist women from the Third World may have actions, even hold a gun to their oppressors, but not thought, nor strategy, nor any systemic demands for women of the world. Francisca de Haan locates the Cold War historiography in Europe and the United States as the primary silencing mechanism that has erased communist and socialist women from the historical record of women's transnational movements in the twentieth century.[12] The historiographic occlusion of women across the occupied world is compounded by adding racism to that Cold War lens, and reveals an anti-communist historiography at work.

Anti-communism has stolen this story of women's internationalism. We have lost the stories of women, even those like

Coulibaly, who were not members of a communist party. Activists like Coulibaly were not politicized by World War II itself, since resistance to colonial occupation is as old as colonialism. But during this Imperial event, the myth of colonialism's inevitability finally crumbled to dust. The willingness of women like Coulibaly to tear down colonialism through building women's collective strength came from their own conditions of survival. They drew on a central leftist tenet: organize the largest possible numbers of people to become their own leaders, to fulfill their own needs and create their own destinies. Coulibaly's anticolonial internationalism stood too close to the women who were communists. Her vision for freedom from occupation in West Africa was too close to socialism. This proximity rendered her not simply invisible to our memories of mid-century women's activism, but impossible in the lens of anti-communism. African women could not willingly, knowingly choose time-honed collectivist methods or redistributive ideals to demand a completely different world. Nor could African women join with women in Asia, Latin America, and the Caribbean to lead the international women's movement in its vision and its practice. Writing a story of a global, mass-based women's organization, one that sharpened the tools of internationalism to demand an end to patriarchy, to colonialism, to fascism, to racism, to war itself is to write the impossible. The story that cannot have happened. But it did.

CHAPTER ONE

The 1949 Asian Women's Conference in Beijing (People's Republic of China)

A THEORY OF WOMEN'S ANTI-IMPERIALIST PRAXIS

The Asian Women's Conference consolidated a theory for women's internationalism that rippled outward after its end, moving across the member nations of the Women's International Democratic Federation and onto the world stage during the Korean War. The two hundred delegates and guests in 1949 carried with them the knowledge, militancy, and demands of the women who sent them to Beijing. They built this theory of praxis from their shared assessment of imperialism after the Second World War, an imperialism now led by Americans who had catapulted into dominance from the ashes of European colonial hegemony. Over the years between its founding in 1945 and the conference in Beijing in 1949, members of the WIDF sharpened a shared analysis of this new imperialism. From this consensus came the anti-imperialist praxis discussed at the Asian Women's Conference, and WIDF members mobilized this praxis to oppose the US-led military onslaught against Korea in the 1950s.

Struggles against colonialism and the newly dominant American imperialism lay at the center of women's internationalism for good reason. The women on the imperialist frontlines of capitalism were at its cutting edge. They were also the global majority; simply put, colonized and occupied territories were where the masses were. The Asian Women's Conference as a postwar origin for their organizational theory opens the possibility for a genealogy for internationalist left feminism that is quite distinct from the international feminisms led by women from Europe and North America. Since the beginning of the twentieth century, women activists from Asian and North African countries had pushed for Western women's anti-imperialist solidarity with virtually no support among international women's organizations. Only after the end of the Second World War did that solidarity seem to find open ears; yet the lesson demanded a clear analysis of imperialism as well as a stubborn politics of location for different women's activism. Internationalist left feminism as it emerged in this period was led from what we sometimes call the Global South—a euphemism for those countries held captive to colonial exploitation. The women who fought colonialism where it struck the hardest developed this internationalist left feminism without euphemism or apology.

The ideological shift within the WIDF during this period is significant. At its inception in 1945, participants from Asian and North African colonies successfully added anti-colonialism to anti-fascism and anti-racism in WIDF's final platform for action. By 1949, WIDF's internationalist praxis went far beyond symbolic solidarity and called for all women's active confrontation of imperialism at home and in the world. For women in colonies and former colonies, the call to action was twofold: build a regional unity among the largest numbers of women, and join the armed resistance against colonialism. For women in imperialist countries, this praxis demanded women's direct refusal of the domestic economy of imperialist militarism and colonial occupation. This double anti-imperialist strategy, attendant to women's differences of resources and access to citizenship, was only one strand of revolutionary feminism within WIDF at this time. Another dominant strategy was that of revolutionary motherhood, mobilized by prosocialist women's movements during the same period of time. Both of these strategies were popular front strategies—that is, strategies developed to widen the women's movement and increase the reach of WIDF's coalition for women around the world. For a while in the 1940s and 1950s, these two strategies were intertwined within the international leftist women's movement.

Revolutionary motherhood was a strategy described by scholars Suzy Kim and Jacqueline Castledine as a bridge to cross the divides of socialism, colonialism, capitalism and imperialism that isolated women in their Cold War factions.[1] On the face of it, this unifying language of revolutionary motherhood should have been antagonistic to the strategy of anti-colonialism that sharply defined the differences between socialism and capitalism. Revolutionary maternalism was not an idealized state of being, or the deification of women's natural place in the reproduction of labor. Instead, the term sought to make a world possible where women *could* choose to be mothers and not sacrifice their lives of their children to war and starvation. Motherhood, in this sense, was an explicitly political subjectivity, a location for social change, for activism and for struggle. But motherhood as a site for political subjectivity was still an aspiration based on this presumed reproductive commonalty among women of the world. It emphasized the role of motherhood as one universal to all women. These two strategies had starkly different registers and modes of address to anti-imperialist women around the world, but during this period, they were not antagonistic.

In contrast, the twofold strategy for anti-colonialism explicitly refused universalist language. Imperialism, in the Marxist sense, was capitalism at its "highest stage," and included top-heavy domination by the financial sectors and intercapitalist contests between near-monopoly firms and their countries. Imperialism necessarily produced stark inequities that were class-based, but also relied upon the intensified and differential oppression of women and the theft of labor power from racialized people of the colonies. This strategy required that women acknowledge these differences of geopolitical power in order to choose an active role in the global struggle against colonialism. For a period in the 1940s and 1950s, during the most active decades of the anticolonial movements, the leftist women's movement used both strategies. Revolutionary motherhood was the public, unifying face of their global activism. Their global campaigns for peace provided a megaphone for the demands by women most crushed by imperialist militarism. And, side by side with revolutionary motherhood, the two-part strategy of women's anticolonialism required that women in occupied regions of the world take up arms when necessary, and that women from occupying countries demand the end to wars of counterinsurgency. These two strategies shaped women's solidarity activism throughout the 1950s, even as they generated increasing debate and friction within the WIDF as the 1950s came to a close.

The 1949 Asian Women's Conference successfully brought attention to the brutal injustices of colonial counterinsurgency, from Indonesia to Malaysia, from Vietnam to China, from India to Iran. Perhaps most subversive of all, it shone a spotlight on the colonial oppressors carrying out these scorched-earth wars: Britain, Holland, France, and the United States. More powerfully than ever before, the lie of colonialism as a civilizing mission failed to maintain its persuasive power—even for those enjoying the fruits of colonial extraction. But the conference, early on, also had another goal. It sought to produce an even wider anti-colonial solidarity that included Africa alongside Asia. The terms of WIDF's stated goals for the Asian Women's Conference were consistent: "1. Fight for Peace; 2. Fight for Rights of Women; 3. Fight for Rights of Children."[2] From 1948 onwards, the word "peace" played a weighty role in anti-imperialist struggles. "Peace," in this sense, held a dialectical contradiction of its moment: the Second World War had ended, but colonial wars to regain control over former colonies had intensified. Peace was not solely a women's issue, but women were central to anti-colonial independence struggles. Peace was not a synonym for "socialism." But peace sought a world apart from the constant drumbeat of imperialism; thus, it was a necessary first step towards socialism. As a political demand, peace pointed out the existential dangers of war in order to create a popular front of the world's people against nuclearism and militarism. Second, it showed that capitalism had failed to meet people's human security needs, instead drifting inexorably into warmongering to protect its failed system. Peace was both a project of uniting a range of political forces across the world, and an ideological way to show the political dangers of capitalism.

Each of these agenda items defined a topic for discussion, a field for action. But every strategy, every tactic developed for struggles as volatile as those across Asia and Africa also demanded a conjunctural analysis—a common understanding of the world to clarify the conditions of leftist activism. Which conditions are specific to a struggle in a particular location? Which are more generalized? Experiential lessons from struggles around the world formed the backbone for both their conjunctural analysis of the present moment and for their movement's strategies and tactics. It framed their debates about what to do next, and how to draw more women into their movement.

ORIGINS OF THE ASIAN WOMEN'S CONFERENCE

The women's internationalist praxis solidified at the Asian Women's Conference began before the December 1945 founding of the host organization, the Women's International Democratic Federation. The Asian Women's Conference might not have ever happened without the growing numbers of women like Celestine Coulibaly and many others who dared to address large public rallies, to knock on the doors of their neighbors, or to take up arms to fight imperialism. In the 1930s, independence movements in many parts of the occupied world shifted from symbolic attacks to mass actions, and both forms of struggle were enacted by women. From the turn of the twentieth century, powerful symbolic attacks against colonialism included raids of colonial weaponry or bombings of the arteries of capital, such as railroads or telegraph stations, by small, revolutionary cells of people.

Beginning in the 1920s, Marxists and other leftists in occupied territories turned towards organizing the largest numbers of people possible through peasant unions, agricultural worker unions, student groups, and women's groups. These mass organizations, as they were called, were ideologically quite open, cohering around widely shared goals. By design, they did not require affiliation to a communist party. They built the confidence of working class and agricultural people that their voice, their demands mattered and could shape the world. Public protests in mass organizations made visible the unity among disparate groups of people against occupation, exploitation, and submission. Mass-based organizing methods joined the discontent of middle-class people with colonial rule to the refusal by working class and peasant people to submit to immiseration and starvation at the hands of large landowners, regional business owners as well as colonial rulers. These mass-based politics put the demands by working class and agricultural workers first rather than last.

Women, particularly rural and working-class women, became one important section for concerted political organization in communist-led and leftist movements. Women joined and initiated these movements because of their universal commitments to full equality for all women and emancipation from feudal, patriarchal customs that shortened women's lives and stole their autonomy. Leftist, and particularly communist, movements directed their focus to the rural areas of colonized regions, the profit-making centers of colonialism. Colonial profits circuited through the cities, which provided efficient transport of rural wealth to the colonial homelands. But urban centers, even those with strong refining industries of coal processing, iron smelting, or jute-weaving were not the primary sources of value extraction for colonialism. Colonial profits were wrung from the back-breaking labor of peasants and the richness of the land itself; profits came from exported agricultural products, trees cut by rural workers, and mineral wealth dug by rural laborers. Mass-based rural organizing in the continents of Asia and Africa struck back at the very heart of colonial power.

ORGANIZING WOMEN UNDER COLONIAL OCCUPATION

Beginning in the 1940s, the mass organization of leftist women in these regions took an important turn towards an internationalist horizon. At the instigation of the Soviet Union, women in leftist national independence movements heeded a call to create anti-fascist organizations that were open to all interested women.[3] The English-language pamphlet distributed globally, *To Women the World Over,* carried speeches from the Women's Anti-Fascist conference held in Moscow on September 7, 1941. Testimonies were filled with gruesome stories of German soldiers' rape of girls and women both in Germany and on battlefronts in Hungary and the Soviet Union.[4] Often operating as coalitions that brought together disparate nationalist women's groups, these anti-fascist women's organizations in colonized countries allowed leftist independence movements to link local struggles for affordable food to women's active fight against fascism. In locations where fascists and fascist allies took over occupation from colonizers, such as Vietnam and Indonesia, the fight for independent territorial control by local people merged seamlessly into the anti-fascist war.

Historian Soma Marik draws from interviews with Indian communist women leaders of this period who described the class-based demand for self-defense from fascism. Leaders of the Mahila Atmaraksha Samiti (MARS), or Women's Self-Defense Organization, emphasized its role in conceiving women as political actors in their own right. "The demand for women's self-defense was posed as a part of the defense against fascism," Marik writes. "As Bani Dasgupta's interview makes clear, women also had to learn to fend for themselves and self-defense was linked to social goals. Notwithstanding persistent talks about honor, the crucial shift was in the insistence that women had to learn to fend for themselves and this defense was linked to social (class) goals."[5] In communist and leftist movements, women's self-defense organizations supported women to "stand straight," in Dasgupta's phrase—that is, to stand as an individual and fight for greater class and social goals.[6] The communist movement in India provided the space for women to forge a political and social identity separate from that given them by their family and by the state. It was this independent identity that allowed women to be active participants, even leaders, in the collectivity of class politics.

By 1943, war-led famines struck across the grain fields of European-dominated territories. The French Vichy government sent wheat from Morocco and Algeria to Europe, devastating the local populations who grew and harvested it. Similarly, the British commandeered India's rice crops. By 1943, the famine had devastated Bengal. The objectives of the anti-fascist women's self-defense organization changed. Renu Chakravartty, a communist founder of MARS, defined their new objective as "defense of the people from starvation and death."[7] Another leader, Manikuntala Sen, described the work by MARS members in Kolkata:

> Dividing time into shifts, some of us would stay near the queues. Procurers from the sex trade would hover around young women who had to be safeguarded. Some women would give birth while they waited and they would have to be looked after. Sometimes a woman would remain in the queue with a dead child in her lap, refusing to let go of her place; there were many such incredible sights. Day and night, our workers didn't have a spare moment.[8]

Large landowners hoarded grain as prices for rice and wheat tripled and quadrupled in the almost empty markets. The Japanese occupation of Burma shut down the usual importation of rice from Burma and Thailand. The British government bought up food staples at sharply higher prices to feed its soldiers along the front lines of India, and exported the rest to troops around the world. In 1941, Bengal imported 296,000 tons of rice, yet by 1942 the flow had reversed to an exported 185,000 tons.[9] Starvation during these colonial famines was deeply gendered. Men migrated in search of food. Women and children were left behind in the countryside; vast numbers of them died there. Others finally came to urban centers to sell what they could for food. Women's internationalism in the colonies after the world wars arose in no small part from these colonial-shaped, war-based famines, replicated across occupied land of almost every continent.

Ela Reid, one of the founders of MARS, attended the inauguration of the Women's International Democratic Federation in December 1945. She described how the defense against starvation and death was a contradictory one: during the war, it required their support for the British forces, the very same military that starved and oppressed the people in India. Self-defense against starvation and death also meant protesting the British colonial administration for inadequate food distribution, facing British-controlled firing squads in the streets, fighting off sex traffickers at food distribution centers, and housing the influx of starving rural people to the cities. Yet Indian women's self-defense could not be a military one to protect their own country from aerial bombardment or land invasion, since armed defense threatened British rule.

> We fought constantly against two enemies, dear friends, one on the inside and the other on the outside. Without clothes and without food, our women faced their share of the struggles you have known.

We are part of the larger body of anti-fascist women in the world. The value of this contribution cannot be denied when you, my friends, realize that India lives under a feudal system. Women live oppressed and exploited. Nevertheless peasants, workers, housewives and intellectuals are willingly anti-imperialist and anti-fascist.[10]

Ela Reid introduced an inside/outside strategy of two enemies, the patriarchal norms and customs of feudalism that closed the horizons for women and girls, and the greed of capitalism that profited from women's marginalization, particularly of working-class, oppressed-caste, and other minoritized women. The two enemies, inside and outside, strengthened each other; the fight against them, thus, had to be twofold. Other delegates who echoed her analysis of the two enemies of feudalism and capitalism included Thelma Dale, the leader of the militant National Negro Congress, and Duong The Hauh, a member of the pro-communist Vietnamese Women's Union of Paris. Together, they transformed popular theories of women's internationalism in the 1940s.[11]

1945: INAUGURATING THE WOMEN'S INTERNATIONAL DEMOCRATIC FEDERATION

In late November 1945, when the Women's International Democratic Federation emerged from the ashes of World War II on principles of world peace, women's rights, democracy, anti-fascism, and children's welfare, 850 participants from forty countries attended its first gathering in Paris, France. Joining WIDF was an organizational, not an individual act, and the list of attendees provides women's names, their country of origin, and their organizational affiliation. Participants were not all communist-linked mass organizations. In fact, many of them were more ideologically jumbled, including those that emerged from the call for women's unified activism against fascism. Four women from India attended their founding Congress, including Ela Reid from MARS.[12] One of them, Vidya Munsi, traveled to Paris directly after the conference of the World Federation of Democratic Youth, another communist-linked mass organization that was held in London the month before. "Over 15,000 women filled the Velodrome D'Hiver (Winter Stadium) to capacity," remembered Munsi of the founding address by French resistance leader Eugenie Cotton, who led the international women's organization from 1945 to 1967.[13]

In 1945, WIDF was the only transnational women's organization that explicitly condemned colonialism and demanded international solidarity for liberation struggles. Its founding document stated: "The Congress calls on all democratic women's organizations of all countries to help the women of the colonial and dependent countries in their fight for economic and political rights." Activists from Vietnam and India in particular, but also the United States and Egypt, deepened WIDF's opening commitments both theoretically and politically. They pushed delegates to define fascism in relationship to imperialism. They described fascism and its racialized genocide as one powerful force behind military conflict. They argued that colonial occupation and anti-black violence were other forms of fascistic violence that crushed the freedom of people around the world. Ela Reid, Jaikishore Handoo, Duong The Hauh, and other delegates made arguments powerful enough to shift the position of delegations like the one from Algeria, in 1945 made up primarily of French-origin, mostly communist members who lived in North Africa.

Duong The Hauh, an expatriate from Vietnam who lived in France, tethered anti-fascism to anti-colonialism. She radically decentered Europe by naming another inside/outside contradiction laid bare during the war.

> Mothers and spouses from Europe, Czechoslovakia, Poland, Russia, France, you who suffered the atrocities committed by the bloodthirsty brutes of Nazism, you who lived next to the crematoriums in Belsen and Maidanek, you learned how far human cruelty can go when an odious regime allows a group of declassed, ambitious, predatory men to indulge freely and entirely into their wild beasts' instincts.
>
> And if the bloodiest drama could unfold this way in Europe, if the most cruel and barbarous actions could be committed by the most civilized countries of the globe, it is because even before this war, even during peacetime, this barbarity already existed there at a latent state, it has always existed, in real and permanent ways in the colonies.
>
> We are, us Indochinese, a colonized people for eighty years. We have been knowing for eighty years a perpetual regime of occupation, oppression, police terror, that reduces human beings to the level of a beast.[14]

Duong The Hauh reminded her audience that inside Europe, anti-Semitism drove the horror of mass incarceration and the murder of Jewish and also Roma people as racialized, religious threats to a homogenous white Christian Europe. Outside Europe, she argued, colonialism was a racialized system of expropriation of land, lives, and resources; as such, it preceded the anti-Semitic holocaust of the mid-twentieth century. "Civilization" references Europe's self-image as well as its fig-leaf rationalization of colonial occupation, extraction of resources, and monopoly over the markets of non-Europe. For Duong The Hauh, the barbarous civilization inside Europe had been integral to its colonial occupations outside Europe for decades, for centuries. Any anti-fascism that was truly integral to women's internationalism must know its history and take stock of its roots. Colonialism was Europe's exterior face of imperialist civilization/barbarity, she argued, and could not possibly remain on the margins of women's internationalism any longer.

The inside/outside solidarity of anti-fascist women in colonized countries had its mirror in the United States, the emergent imperial global power after the war ended. Thelma Dale was an African American woman who laid tracks for radical civil rights organizing before and after the end of World War II. One of the key founders of the Southern Negro Youth Congress, as well as the National Negro Congress, Dale defined an inside/outside from within the United States—one that forged a method of organizing similar to that described by Ela Reid. "We, Negro women of the United States," she said, "despite the fact that we did not have and do not yet have the full enjoyment of our rights as citizens that our white sisters have, we recognized what we are risking in the war against fascism and we have contributed with all our might. Through our efforts, we helped win the war. But now we must continue the struggle against fascism and fascist tendencies, in our country as well as abroad."[15] Struggles against systemic racist disenfranchisement continued during the war, similar to the self-defense against starvation and death fought by women in India during the war. Even without full citizenship rights inside the United States, Dale placed anti-colonial solidarity at the center of Black American women's internationalism. "(W)e actively participate in mass demonstrations and any action to pressure our government so that it does not touch China and that our American soldiers return home," she told the other delegates. "We actively encourage the struggle of the Indonesian people for freedom and the efforts that other people in India, Africa, Puerto Rico and elsewhere are making to regain their freedom."[16]

As women from the United States, they countered US aggression in China against the communist Red Army. They supported the right to self-determination for Puerto Rico, a US colony. After its founding conference, the WIDF leadership decided to prioritize gathering information about women's conditions in colonized countries in order to strengthen ties between WIDF and anti-racist and anti-colonial women's movements like Dale's.

In 1945, WIDF organizers had not yet made inroads with revolutionary African women residing in Paris. Adeline Broussan reminds us that women from across the French-occupied territories of Africa lived in Paris in 1945, so travel restrictions after the war do not fully explain why the African delegates were all from North Africa.[17] As Katharine McGregor shows, women's participation in anti-occupation, anti-fascist movements in this region was active and growing.[18] The WIDF's founding conference also remained silent about the French troops' massacre of thousands of Algerians who joined the independence demonstrations in Constantinois from May to July, 1945. The Algerian delegation in 1945 did not support the end of French colonialism in North Africa. Alice Sportisse stated their position unequivocally: "Women of our country agree with the principles of the Atlantic Charter that stands in favor of the right of all peoples to self-determination. But it is clear that they understand that it is not in Algeria's interest to ask for divorce from the new, democratic France...."[19]

Communist women from occupied French countries, including Algeria and Morocco, held out hope for the left-led French government immediately after the war ended. But that hope was short-lived. It took one long year for the Algerian members to categorically denounce colonialism and build their membership among Muslim Algerian women. In October 1946, the Algerian delegate Jeanne Merens delivered her report about colonialism and racism to the WIDF executive committee. She described the end of French occupation as the only answer to the famine devastating the people of Algeria: "It is necessary to strike at the root of this evil, the cause is none other than the colonial system."[20] It took a little longer to include sub-Saharan African women in their meetings, and this development was built from travel by WIDF international committee members to meet with anti-colonial women's groups in West Africa, East Africa, and Southern Africa. In 1948, the Union of Women of Abeokuta in Nigeria sought and gained membership in WIDF.

A women's group did not have to be communist-affiliated to join the federation. But even with its open political character, those groups that joined WIDF chose a known proximity to communist parties and the wider communist movements. The heart of WIDF's goals for women's emancipation, as well its commitment to a political eclecticism, were part of an older leftist tradition. They espoused Marxist-Leninist theories for social transformation that were based in a commitment to the masses of people, and sought socialist ideals for a liberatory world order. WIDF's opening call to action against colonialism gained strength and clarity over the next three years with the active participation of their members from Asia and Africa. Due to concerted interventions by these members, the struggles against fascism, racism, and colonialism became integrated into the struggle against imperialism.

1946–1947: FACT-FINDING ABOUT RACISM AND IMPERIALISM

In the immediate aftermath of WIDF's founding conference, three members were designated to convene and develop a report on racism and colonial oppression: Jaikishore Handoo from India,

Vivian Carter Mason from the United States, and Jeanne Merens from Algeria. Also in 1946, the vice-president of WIDF, Marie-Claude Vaillant-Couturier traveled to Argentina, Chile, Brazil, and Uruguay to meet with women movement leaders in Latin America. On her tour she attended the founding of the Brazilian Women's Union. At the first session of the WIDF council, held in February 1947, Handoo reiterated the contradictions within the language of peace and freedom mobilized by social democrats and the newly forming United Nations. This language of peace and freedom was certainly aspirational, but it did not go far enough to support anti-colonial struggles. "Freedom," stressed Handoo, "is indivisible. As long as there are remnants of fascism and imperialism, there can be no peace for humanity and all plans to build a new world, seductive as they are, will be in vain."[21] Handoo's criticism gained support from Ana Pauker, the Romanian delegate. "We must ask the question of solidarity with the people and women in the colonial countries," Pauker stated. "We must now denounce and explain to women and people how to fight against oppression and colonial domination."[22]

In October 1947 the WIDF leadership established fact-finding in South and Southeast Asia as the organization's "primary concern."[23] They planned to tour Vietnam and Indonesia as well as India, Malaya, and Burma in early 1948. The Dutch and the French governments denied the delegation visas to enter their colonies, however, so the visit was limited to the three countries under British rule: India, Malaya, and Burma. In March and April, 1948, four women from WIDF visited these countries and wrote a damning assessment of how colonialism had systematically impoverished the people.[24] Based in part on their report, WIDF published "The Women of Asia and Africa," addressing Asian women directly. "The importance of your struggle is tremendous for the development of democracy in your respective countries and ... in the world, for the weakening of the imperialist forces of the war-mongers," they wrote. "The WIDF affirms to our sisters in Asia that it will support their struggle by fighting against the imperialist forces."[25]

1947–1948: PREPARATIONS FOR THE ASIAN WOMEN'S CONFERENCE

Asian activists had, for several years, felt the need for a pan-Asian anti-imperialist women's meeting. Women at the frontlines of the communist movement in India attended the Asian Relations Conference, held in Delhi in 1947. The ARC, as Carolien Stolte describes, brought together world leaders who sought independence on their own terms.[26] Nationalist women attended the main sessions and participated actively in the discussions. They also met for some women-only conversations to focus on specific issues like women's economic independence and social issues. Communist women like Hajrah Begum from India played important roles in the discussions, but this gathering did not quench their thirst for more trenchant critiques of colonialism and a more robust socialist horizon. WIDF shared the hopes of these Asian militant women for more than simply national independence from colonial power. The organization also had the capacity in terms of staff, resources, and time to host an Asian Women's Conference that would allow activists to build networks that went beyond their shared support for anti-colonial struggles in the region. Leftist women sought to overturn capitalist and feudal exploitation and oppression after national independence.

The head of the preparatory committee for the Asian Women's Conference was Lu Cui. Between 1947 and 1950, Cui worked

Figure 2. Lu Cui and Marie-Claude Vaillant-Couturier at the World Peace Conference, 1951. Photo courtesy of Sophia Smith Archives, Smith College.

for WIDF in its central office in Paris, acting as WIDF's international liaison for women's movements across Africa and Asia. Cui joined the Chinese Communist Party in the 1930s when she fought against Japanese occupation as a student in Beijing. Before the Communist Party of China (CPC) victory in 1949, the Party sent Cui to hold this senior post in WIDF, an indication of how seriously they took their membership in WIDF. By 1948, Cui was a member of the standing committee of the All-China Democratic Women's Federation (later called the All-China Women's Federation) and the secretary of WIDF. She was an obvious choice to be the secretary general of the Conference's preparatory committee.

Originally the Asian Women's Conference was supposed to be held in Kolkata, India, in October 1948. Cui traveled to Kolkata early in 1948 to advise members of MARS during their unsuccessful efforts to organize the conference. Euro-American pressure on Nehru's government in India, and his government's distrust of Indian communism as a destabilizing force in the country, undermined those plans. The revolutionary focus of discussions of the World Federation of Democratic Youth in Asia, held in Kolkata in February 1948, further sealed the government's decision not to allow another radical gathering of anti-imperialist activists. After her failure to convince Indian officials to support the Asian Women's Conference, Cui wondered, "how we should interpret the government's refusal to host a conference that would treat many issues crucial to Asian women?"[27] Her implied answer was obvious and disappointing. Even newly independent governments, like the one in India, with its strong nationalist tradition of supporting women's rights, did not care enough. The Asian Relations Conference held in Delhi in 1947, with its poorly-attended women-only sessions, was acceptable to Nehru's government. A pan-Asian women's conference on the communist left was not, so they would have to look elsewhere.

WIDF organizers considered invitations from Indonesia and Vietnam before accepting China's invitation to hold the conference there. The *Information Bulletin* enthusiastically announced the final venue in June 1949, on the heels of the founding of the People's Republic of China. "The triumphant victories of the New China have proven that neither dollars, nor planes, nor tanks are justification for a people who want to live in freedom."[28] The Asian Women's Conference was framed by this triumph as "one more victory that the oppressed people in struggle will win, it is a victory for all the action of women all over the world in their common effort for democracy and peace."[29]

The CIA also paid close attention to the preparations for the conference.[30] They noted the preparatory meetings held in Shanghai, Beijing, Changsha, Tianjin, Hangzhou, and the

Shaanxi-Gansu-Ningxia border region. The CIA report listed the elected delegates' names, and provided the total number of Chinese delegates to the conference as 110 women. The preparatory committee for the Asian Women's Conference, the CIA report noted, included ten women, from Kirghiz (then part of the Soviet Socialist Republic, not Kyrgyzstan), Korea, Vietnam, India, Burma (now Myanmar), and one delegate each from WIDF's central offices and the Women's Anti-Fascist League of the USSR. They included the detail that the Beijing Women's League asked 209 families to make embroidered tablecloths, bedspreads, and, in one example of the handicraft that returned home with an American delegate, handkerchiefs. Conference funding came from a range of sources: communist parties gave resources and infrastructure, such as the Chinese Communist Party, which helped shoulder the considerable costs of hosting the conference. WIDF members held fundraisers to support delegates' travel costs, with some European sections, particularly the Dutch and the French, sponsoring the travel costs of Asian delegates. The USSR gave additional funds, as did Czechoslovakia, Bulgaria, and a number of socialist states in Eastern Europe.[31]

1948: WIDF'S SECOND CONGRESS OF WOMEN

The momentum for the Asian Women's Conference increased substantially during the Second Congress of Women held by WIDF in Budapest, Hungary. During this gathering of 390 women from fifty-one nations, WIDF released "The Women of Asia and Africa." The report drew from their fact-finding mission to South and Southeast Asia, as well as the communications built up in Africa by Lu Cui and other members of the WIDF network. It described the interconnections of African and Asian women in their resistance to colonialism nationally and imperialism internationally.[32] The Second Congress, with its central focus on anti-imperialism and women's militant politics in Asia and Africa, emphasized the fault lines of women's internationalism in the years after 1945. By 1948, its analysis and commitment to fight for national independence and against imperialism sharpened substantially. The Second Congress's resolution entitled "Development of the Democratic Women's Movement in the Countries of Asia and Africa" gave unvarnished support to anti-imperialist struggles across the continents.[33] The connection between these regions is clear: colonialism. "The imperialists of the United States, Great Britain, France and Holland estimate the change in the balance of forces correctly; they mobilize their armies feverishly to maintain at all costs their profits and privileges, create military and strategic bases, accentuate their repressive methods of government, and resort to making war upon the colonial and semi-colonial countries."[34] This Congress sharpened the organization members' shared analysis of imperialism in the postwar period, even as it spurred clearer disagreements about what strategy they should pursue to organize "women of the world."

Anti-imperialist strategies and conjunctural analyses of colonialism had developed for decades; for one example, see the School for Peoples of the East held in Moscow and Guangzhou. Theories of organizing traveled among other spheres of pro-socialist organizing, in no small part because activists at WIDF attended multiple gatherings, including radical student organizations like the International Union of Studies (IUS), the World Federation of Democratic Youth (WFDY), and the World Federation of Trade Unions (WFTU). Women and girls were in all of these formations: as students, as youth and as workers. One central conjunctural question debated fiercely in all of these circles was the changing character of financial capitalism, and more specifically, the role of the United States as the newest, and, for this moment at least, the most powerful banker at the end of World War II. But WIDF, as the organization for pro-socialist women, developed another central question for the larger movement: what is a gendered conjunctural analysis of the moment? In Budapest, at their Second Women's Congress, WIDF members provided this analysis about the character of financial capitalism and US imperialism. In 1948, they also began to further shape their answer to another vital question. Given this conjunctural analysis of imperialism, what were women's roles in the struggle? They articulated why "peace" held powerful stakes for anti-imperialist women's activism in the second half of the twentieth century.

CONJUNCTURAL ANALYSIS OF US IMPERIALISM

Cai Chang summed up the politically transformative moment of the postwar world of 1948 in one blunt assessment. "In the course of the last three years, American imperialism has supplanted the imperialism of other countries in the colonies."[35] She delivered her analysis of imperialism and the people's anti-imperialism late in the WIDF's Second Congress on Women, held in Budapest, Hungary over six days in December 1948. Cai was a leader in the Communist Party of China—and many of the delegates who attended this conference were also leading members in their communist parties. Cai also held many roles in WIDF: she was a member of the Congress organizing committee, a new vice president voted into office during the Congress, and an integral member of the preparatory committee for the upcoming Conference of the Women of Asia. Even with independence battles raging across Asia, everyone at the conference agreed, colonialism was in its violent death throes as the preeminent form of capitalist imperialism.

Over the twentieth century, new imperialist tools had been sharpened by the United States, and these had gained dominance after 1945. American imperialism had specific characteristics that delegates from Latin America, North Africa, the Caribbean, and Asia assessed from hard-won experience. Europe was newly at its mercy, as delegates from France particularly decried. The United States was the true victor of World War II, gaining a hegemony won through its capital reconstruction loans to Europe and England. Yet Cai's advice to the gathering of internationalist women urged them to stay the course on anti-imperialist organizing: develop unity among the working class, peasants, and oppressed people across rural and urban landscapes. Fight for universal rights for women and marginalized people as a whole. Demand a just peace across the globe. And build a world that provides economic security for all. Cai and other delegates stressed that unity among the masses of organized women around the world was the backbone of WIDF's strength.

Cai began her address reminding her audience of their new gains. "Many countries have passed out of the capitalist system. The States of People's Democracy arose. The front of the progressive forces, with the great Soviet Union at its head, is enlarged and strengthened."[36] American imperialism had gained ascendance, but the global war had catalyzed areas for liberatory possibility as well. Countries like Hungary, Poland, and Czechoslovakia became socialist republics at the close of the war. Their active support for a world socialist movement joined with the USSR and in solidarity with national liberation and socialist movements was a welcome new development. Cai joined the gathering in Budapest during some of the CPC Red Army's heaviest fighting, against forces led by the Guomindang and backed by the United States with generous loans and military hardware of every kind. Her conjunctural argument about the revolutionary potential for socialism in the middle of the twentieth century came from this experience. Communists in China had benefited from Soviet support after the war in material, diplomatic, and military ways at critical moments. By 1948, they had already consolidated rural parts of the country, and had begun to win over the cities as well. They also accepted an influx of Chinese soldiers abandoning the Guomindang forces to join the Red Army. The war within China would not be over for another several months, but Cai predicted an imminent victory for socialism in the face of American imperialism.

Cai paraphrased Lenin for her slogan that echoed throughout many of the speeches: "A people which oppresses another cannot itself be free."[37] This slogan, heard so many times over the six days of the congress, threaded together emergent political strategies. Women across Africa and Asia demanded freedom with peace. European and American women needed to act with equal urgency, though from a distinctly different location. Cai obliquely referenced Andrei Zhdanov's two-camp theory of the postwar order: the capitalist nations' camp was imperialist, the socialist and anticolonial nations' camp was democratic.[38] This doctrine "declared that communist parties were natural leaders of the anticolonial struggle."[39] As such, she bridged the character of anti-imperialist internationalism for the women on the front lines of colonialism and the women still figuring out their role in this battle. Speaking directly to women from imperialist nations, she explained:

This must be the slogan under which the Union of French Women fights to strengthen the struggle against the war in Vietnam.... The women of Holland must ceaselessly demand the cessation of the colonial war, and the recall of the troops from Indonesia. This slogan must also be adopted by women of the other imperialist countries, above all those of the United States. They must help their sisters *not only because they are moved by a sentiment of justice, but because the struggle of the women in the dependent countries against the oppressors is part of the fight for peace and democracy.* Our American sisters must demand the retreat of the American troops from South Korea.[40]

Cai said that women from France, Holland, and the United States must lead an anti-imperialist campaign for peace. She urged women in imperialist nations to become *accomplices* in struggle, not simply allies to colonized women. This solidarity had consequences, and women paid them in full.

In the Marxist-Leninist tradition mapping the contradictions of global capitalism, Cai detailed the new contours of imperialism in the years after the Second World War. She drew lessons for the global women's movement that extended beyond the war in China, and linked its struggle with that faced by all colonized territories against colonial power. "The crisis of the colonial system, which is expressed in a powerful movement of national liberation in the colonies and dependent countries of Asia and Africa. This movement threatens the basis of the entire capitalist system."[41] Colonialism was in crisis, she stated, and the recent world war had exacerbated this crisis. Additionally, Cai stated, by 1948, the crisis of colonialism shook the foundations of capitalism itself. In one of the last reports at the Budapest conference, Cai made an argument that women's internationalist support for national independence movements should be at the center of WIDF's work for women's rights. Cai's argument about imperialism in 1948 formed the backbone of anti-colonial organizing from the early twentieth century. Her answer to why anti-colonial movements had gained such unprecedented success after the end of the world war in 1945 was new, since so many of the relations of violence and exploitation continued unabated. Colonial powers' use of violent force to maintain control had not lessened one iota; if anything, it was fiercer than before the war. The economies of the Netherlands, England, and France still relied upon colonies' wealth in resources, labor and captive consumer markets—perhaps even more desperately in the war's aftermath. The reason brute force and bad-faith agreements to share power no longer sufficed, Cai said, was the unification of wide cross-sections of the masses of working people and educated middle-class people that she designated as "progressive forces of the country."[42]

This unity against colonialism, solidified by the war, centered the militant crucible of people's movements against capitalism in Asia and Africa. Cai argued in her 1948 address that these liberation movements were not isolated battles of desperate women and men across the globe; since together, they refused the foundations of colonialism and thus challenged the viability of capitalism itself. She linked movements in Africa, including labor struggles in the Gold Coast, to those in Asia, citing the oil workers' strikes in Iran. She spoke about the food shortages in China that led to peasant uprisings against the Guomindang, and the starvation in India that fueled peasant resistance to large landowners in Bengal. All of these struggles included women workers on the land and in factories, exploited more intensively by lower wages and longer hours. While Cai spoke about the exploitation of both women and men, her focus on women's lives in colonialism was clear: working women's demands should ground anticolonial demands, as the floor that would change the oppressive living conditions for all.

Cai assessed the anti-imperialist moment through the growing numbers of militant struggles for freedom. "After the war," Cai said, "the national independence movement in the countries of Asia and Africa has won unprecedented victories. Armed struggle is at present the characteristic feature of this movement."[43] Those rural and urban movements created an immoveable wall in support of anti-colonial guerilla wars fought with little weaponry in the name of the vast numbers of colonized people. She advocated coalitions across nationalist women's groups, coalitions that drew middle class, working class and agricultural women into the revolutionary women's movement. Her advice was not always possible, even within Asia with its well-developed anti-colonial movements. In the mid-1940s, leftist Indian women faced expulsion from the largest women's organization in India, the All India Women's Commission (AIWC), because of their commitment to organizing rural and urban working class and poor women. In addition, both the old European form of imperialism and the new American form agreed to use military solutions for "wiping out every movement for national liberation."[44] Delegates to WIDF's Second Congress fully supported Cai's unapologetic embrace of armed freedom movements as the necessary response to colonial nations' military aggression and the occupation of land and people for profit.

ECONOMICS, WOMEN'S RIGHTS, AND PEACE

Over the six days of WIDF's Second International Congress of Women in 1948, delegates explored how American imperialism functioned and how the United States had gained the upper hand over Europe. Out of this analysis, they developed a way for women of the world to demand imperialism's end. The end of militarism. Simply put, peace. The end of profiting from others' misery. Peace. The end of the shrunken roles for women as keepers of the home. Peace. Together, over the six days of the conference, delegates from around the world sharpened their analysis of American imperialism to better measure its form, its strengths, and most importantly, its contradictions and weaknesses. WIDF's second conference still lacked significant representation from most of Africa. The report from the Transvaal Women's Union of South Africa, an early multiracial women's group led by Black South African women, was extensive. They highlighted the severity of South Africa's segregation and the depths of Black South Africans' economic exploitation. Members were not allowed to travel to Budapest—no passports, no visas—but their analysis and their courage entered the conference. Together, delegations and reports from around the world sought to build the strongest women's internationalist movement possible.

From the very beginning, the women who joined the Women's International Democratic Federation agreed on the shared core precept that women's rights and women's emancipation from bondage, oppression, and exploitation require a world at peace. Peace, in this sense, is not simply a temporal state of not-being-at-war. Peace is a process of social organization sustained by cultures and ideologies of mutually beneficial coexistence and support that allowed everyone to thrive. Kutty Hookham, a conference guest from the World Federation of Democratic Youth, described it thus: "peace is not a passive state."[45] At the heart of WIDF members' definition, peace is also an economics, and that economics requires socialism. Their language is condensed in their official reports and resolutions, but consistent.

> The 2nd International Congress of Women calls on all of the national organizations of the Federation to intensify their struggle for a lasting peaceand for friendship between the peoples—the struggle against the instigators of a new war, against fascism and for democratic liberties and national independence for all peoples, against intervention by the imperialists in the internal affairs of other countries, against colonial slavery.[46]

This resolution has a call for anti-imperialist and anti-fascist action embedded in its analysis of the political economics of its time. National liberation was not additional to the struggle for women's rights in the 1940s, it was the necessary cornerstone (albeit no guarantee) of women's access to full political and economic rights. The WIDF's consensus resides in other key terms repeated again and again in their publications. For instance, that fascism is the blunt end of capitalism, the tool to forcibly take land, enforce the peoples' submission and, thus, greater profits. Or that imperialism is the current and "highest" stage of capitalist development, to use Lenin's description, and that imperialism is not a synonym for colonialism; that is, imperialism is not simply the political capture of markets and resources, but it refers to the monopolistic relations of finance capitalism, relations which can take many forms.

The delegates that most sharply defined this newly hegemonic iteration of finance capitalism during the conference were all from colonized, formerly-colonized, or, in the language of the day, semi-colonized countries. Lu Cui, alongside Cai Chang, shared her knowledge of this new imperialism, one that had developed new levers of control, as well as new methods of monopolizing power and wealth across the globe. Lu Cui provided a detailed account of American imperialism in China during the direct attack against the Chinese Communist Party forces by the Guomindang beginning in 1946. For the first time in China, US expansionism acted alone with no competition from European powers. The US government provided the Guomindang forces with their full military support, including equipment and loans worth five billion dollars. She detailed how the required payback for their support went beyond interest payments on the debt, and revealed the hidden imperial sinews of the bargain. The United States got priority rights in all resource extraction, as well as building railroads and shipping facilities. They held the rights over the finance and administration of these holdings. Under the guise of providing military advisors, the United States seized the entirety of the Guomindang's air and naval bases. But Lu Cui's description had a happy ending. The Americans had lost all of these assets, and all of their control over China. "The Chinese people have fully and completely smashed the American imperialist plot to enslave them!"[47]

Delegates from Europe, such as the French General Assembly and communist party member Jeannette Vermeersch, excoriated the Marshall Plan as "a poverty plan" that sought to leach the wealth from and sovereignty of from war-ravaged European nations.[48] Edith Buchaca, a leading member of the Communist Party of Cuba, reminded the Europeans of the precursors to the Marshall Plan in the Caribbean and Latin America: "the regime which is now being exported to Europe under the name of 'relief' has pillaged Latin America above all.... The Marshall Plan is to Europe what the Clayton Plan is to Latin America. However, Washington does not even consider that it is under any obligation to offer relief in the question of Latin America."[49] The lessons of economic colonialism, through debt and development, were shared as they moved from Latin America to Europe in this period. But the material gains already hoarded in

Europe meant that the long-term effects would not be identically borne by the people on these continents.

Even when exporting loan and purchasing agreements to Europe, American imperialism followed racist logics, with some forms of debt relief for war loans taken in Europe, but none in Latin America. Olga Luzardo was a leader within the Communist Party of Venezuela. The funds for her trip to the Women's Congress in Budapest were raised by the women and men who worked in the oil fields. She used the example of the United States' rationing of iron processing machines to maintain her country's economic dependence. "We have iron—we have not yet calculated what quantities. Venezuelans know that we could well make plans for its utilization; but the machines which come from North America are rationed in such a way as to prevent our processing large quantities, goods which it is interested in placing on our markets."[50] Luzardo described the US government's calculated decision to withhold industrial technology to Latin America. These familiar features of European colonialism, of economic underdevelopment to maintain captive markets, still operated in the American version. A brutally enforced "comparative advantage" hadn't changed since the times of David Ricardo.

Fanny Edelman, a communist from Argentina, repeated the question in her report, "Who is threatening Latin America if not imperialism?" She listed the sinews of American imperialism during the twentieth century that pipelined the profits by their industries northward, from meatpacking to cotton production to cold storage. Massive direct investment by US firms fostered Argentina's industrial underdevelopment, and led to the long-term transfer of Argentinian capital to the United States as profits and dividends. Autocratic political control of US imperialism "made Panama a strategic base for America, which is the master of Puerto Rico, which had the leaders of the Cuban working class assassinated and which is trying to unseat the democratic government of Venezuela."[51] War, profits and control linked the Marshall Plan "for economic domination" to the Truman Plan "for organizing a continent-wide army under American orders, with the establishment of air, naval and land bases in Latin America. They were "two aspects of the same imperialist policy."[52]

Edelman's litany spanned every corner of Latin America and the Caribbean to detail the armed militarism wielded to enforce American economic and political hegemony in the region—until the dragon's tail met its mouth—when economic coercion co-opted the region's military forces to American ends, with air, naval and land bases across the region. She ended her speech with an answer to "who ... if not imperialism?": "But we reply to the imperialists ... that the time of oppression is gone. We who had songs of liberty for our lullabies remain faithful to our history of freedom."[53] The analysis of the full range of delegates at the Budapest Conference created a common conjunctural analysis of US imperialism, one that fostered their strategies of resistance as they sought a richer, stronger women's internationalism.

THE ASIAN WOMEN'S CONFERENCE

Given the immense difficulty of the process, why hold a separate conference for Asian women who were fighting military battles for independence? Why not simply build women's organizations around the region to gather their strength first? Pham Ngoc Thuan, the Vietnamese delegate to the Second Congress in 1948, voiced her aspirations for the Asian Women's Conference. "We strongly hope that the exchange of views between the delegates of the different countries of Asia, the experiences of the peoples in their struggles, will help the Congress to work out resolutions which will ensure energetic support to the resistance movement of the women of Asia."[54] Her hopeful words were more than a gesture. Embedded in her statement of support is a demand for leadership by Asian women's movements, and the development of strategies for the global movement by drawing from their experiences, their analysis. Asian women and the context of anti-imperialist movements for liberation, she stressed, must sharpen WIDF's conference resolutions.

At the Asian Women's Conference, as Thuan envisioned it, Asian delegates would have a chance to confer with each other and learn about the differences and commonalties in their struggles. These regional ties could only strengthen their movements, since building regional solidarity was a critical tool. But their conference resolutions also sought to bring women from the entire world into more active resistance against imperialism. Separatism of region or of politics would isolate their struggles—Asian women's anti-colonial struggles for independence and women's rights, a pro-socialist vision for their future, required the creation of a global movement. Colonialism wasn't just a burden for the oppressed to bear or to gain international sympathy; here, Thuan chided the expressions of sympathy for colonized women that characterized some of the reports emerging from the 1948 Conference itself.[55] Colonialism, as a systemic tool used to shore up capitalism, excluded no one from its grasp.

As of 1948, WIDF's organizational bodies only had active members from North Africa, primarily Algeria and Morocco, but also Tunisia and Egypt. Lu Cui, Simone Bertrand, and others traveled extensively in Africa, building relationships with African women beyond the Maghreb. The well-known women's rights and anti-colonial activist Funmilayo Ransome-Kuti of

Nigeria was one of the women that they met.⁵⁶ But even as early as 1947, the gears of anti-communism had begun to turn. The connections between WIDF and communist parties around the world, including the USSR, was undeniable. Many of WIDF's members were not communists; but most of its leaders were communist party members. Ransome-Kuti was invited to the 1949 Asian Women's Conference, but due to her wariness of communism, she decided not to attend. Others did, such as Gisele Rabesahala from Madagascar, Baya Allaouchiche from Algeria, and, as we have seen, Celestine Ouezzin Coulibaly from Ivory Coast. The conference strengthened the horizon of Afro-Asian solidarity as an anti-colonial solidarity, grounded in a vision for women's rights and peace. Ransome-Kuti was ultimately convinced of the WIDF's sincerity to that vision, and became a vice-president in the early 1950s.

Eslanda Robeson attended the Asian Women's Conference as a journalist, sponsored by the Council for African Affairs, the Congress of American Women, and the Progressive Party. She was a member of all of these groups, but rather than attend as a representative of any of them, she described her relationship to the conference as that of a reporter and an eyewitness.⁵⁷ She published a number of articles and delivered many talks about her trip to China and about the conference itself. The articles were published in journals on the left—*Freedom*, started by her husband Paul Robeson, and *New World Review*, the journal coming out of the National Council for American-Soviet Friendship and for the Associated Negro Press. Soon after she returned, she launched a speaking tour that crossed the country to describe what she had learned about the new People's Republic of China, as well as about colonialism, racism, and the united struggle by women around the world for freedom.⁵⁸

Robeson's talks and writings sought to refute dominant representations in the press, and by the US government, representations that shaped (and were shaped by) US foreign policies that targeted communist China as a dangerous force. In seeking to show another perspective, Robeson sought to persuade her audience that another point of view was possible. Like almost every woman who attended the AWC, she came home and immediately began speaking at meetings, writing articles in the press, talking to interested groups, and giving interviews about what she learned. Through talks and articles, Robeson reached out to American women, with a special focus on African American women. In this sense, Robeson, like other AWC delegates, created and spread propaganda. They sought to teach their audiences about the anti-imperialist women's movement, and persuade them that it was a movement worth supporting. In the context of anti-communist countries like the United States, they attempted to dismantle dominant narratives about socialism as a lived political program. But "propaganda" does not just describe a weapon of the weak that seeks to explain another way of seeing the world.

In 1950, Robeson framed her article against the US invasion of Korea through her critique of US government propaganda.[59] She discounted the narrative of President Truman and his administration by parsing the suspect timeline and the supposed decision by the UN Security Council to launch the attack against North Korean troops.[60] The hypocrisy of the United Nations was her next target. "The United Nations, set up to cope with just such an emergency, to negotiate peacefully to prevent wars, or to stop them once they've started, is now itself waging war without even trying to negotiate. In justice to the UN it must be said, however, that only American troops, not UN troops, are fighting Koreans in Korea."[61] Robeson questioned the convenient cover story of the United Nations (rather than the United States) authorizing troops to fight North Korea. She also emphasized the deadly hypocrisy of the United Nations contravening its own mandate to refuse to take sides on partisan conflicts like a civil war. Her article illustrated another kind of propaganda, one wielded by the powerful that operated by other means than persuasion by facts, data, or first-hand witness. John Foster Dulles's characterization of the US war in Korea was the final nail for Robeson: "Our government and the United Nations are not waging war, they are waging peace."[62] Hegemonic propaganda, as Robeson characterized it, mobilizes the register of coercion, a kind of epistemological game of chicken, in this case, over the meaning of war and peace (as Dulles did), rather than bringing reasoned argument, documented facts, or first-hand witness to support its interpretation.

Perhaps most critical to this project, a third register of propaganda circulated during this period that was explicitly anticommunist. Propaganda here refers to a mode of communist and pro-socialist communication. In this sense, propaganda was necessarily a lie, but a silver-tongued one that sought to take in the gullible. In its overview of WIDF from 1945–1954, the British secret service characterized the entire organization as propaganda. "The importance of the Federation's work lies partly in its direct actions, but even more in its value as a propaganda machine.... The message of 'peace' is a profitable line to exploit among women who are unlikely to ponder on the ulterior political significance of exhortations to 'prevent the sending of soldiers to Viet Nam and Malaya, demand the return of sons and husbands, prevent the use of your lands for the storage of arms.' (Resolution of the WIDF Executive Committee, Helsinki, April, 1950)."[63] The WIDF becomes a machine, or perhaps just one cog in the communist machine, that creates propaganda, weaponizing both innocent and not-so-innocent women tricked by its invocations of peace. Women's activism unwittingly works in the favor of the socialist Soviet Union, against the manifest interests of the capitalist West. Propaganda has become a term synonymous with bad-faith lies, almost entirely unmoored from the first, more politically neutral meaning that refers to the widespread dissemination of a perspective or an argument to persuade people.

Propaganda operated in all of these registers during the midtwentieth century: spreading the word as widely and effectively as possible; the brute force of hegemonic narratives to create shared facts; and the siren song, particularly emanating from the USSR, to advance the interests of Marxism and communism. These three uses of "propaganda" require different heuristics, different ways of knowing—and they all circulate in the current context. To testify, to gather facts, to create a convincing narrative and persuade an audience are practices at the heart of journalism. Of academic writing. Of non-fiction. The propaganda of hegemony still requires a whole world of ideological and military strength to function effectively. To lie is a form of power, since being believed is secondary to not being opposed. For this project, the third definition of propaganda is ever-present, lurking around every epistemological corner. My research transforms into propaganda at its first inquiry. That is, to ask what was the Asian Women's Conference suggests that the conference actually occurred; indeed, that it was in fact, a conference of, by, and for Asian women. This is a story that reads archives as propaganda, and understands propaganda as theory. Because the WIDF archives are largely silent about the debates among the delegates at the Asian Women's Conference, its remaining outcomes lie in its most public outcome: the collectively written resolutions and appeals. The inside/outside praxis for women's internationalism that emerged from the Asian Women's Conference in these resolutions and appeals muffles the multiplicity of delegate perspectives into a single collective voice of persuasion, of propaganda.

One reason that prosocialist and anticolonial feminist theory seems impossible is that stock figure of anticommunist history, the dupe. The woman who didn't understand the brutality behind communist promises for equality and mistakenly called herself a communist. The person of color who signed on too easily to communist labor movements, or anti-lynching campaigns, and thus trafficked in communism by inadvertent misunderstanding. The colonized masses who lacked individuals, concrete goals, or theory, were all dupes: that is, uncomprehending masses used by a world communism led by the Soviet Union.

The reading strategy of prosocialist, anticolonial feminist theory as propaganda, in the third sense of the term, anchors anticommunist histories of transnational feminist movements. The racism embedded in the dupe and in "propaganda" as a communist disinformation machine determines the miasma around this history. Taewoo Kim provides a powerful example in his discussion of the accusations lodged against the United States and the United Nations in light of the release of documentation by the United States Air Force. Kim writes, "the value of the report has been completely disregarded and dismissed until now, just as it was during the Korean War. The politics and culture of the Cold War treated the critical statements of the final report of the WIDF Commission (Women's International Commission for the Investigation of War Atrocities Committed in Korea, the official name of the Commission) entirely as pro-Soviet and pro-communist political propaganda."[64] Dismissing anticolonial feminist texts as propaganda wrought by unfortunate dupes of scheming Marxist movements for liberation renders these theories not only invisible, but inconceivable. The erasure is so complete that all memory of anticolonial feminist theories is wiped from the official history of transnational feminism.

This genealogy of a prosocialist internationalist feminism begins with a simple premise: anticolonial, prosocialist women activists from the Third World developed their commitments consciously, analytically, and politically, through their own experience of the world. With this founding premise, "propaganda" emerged as a reading method, rather than a dismissal. A fourth definition for propaganda developed: propaganda as a heuristic that takes seriously *how* theories for transnational feminism emerged from revolutionary anticolonial struggles around the world. Out of this conundrum of missing archives, I developed a method for reading propaganda as a collective voice, one heard most clearly in those official documents and slogans that seem to have no author and many authors. Propaganda as a methodology and historical text is not simply an addition to the usual methods of social history, where personal recollections, including interviews, memoirs, and diaries, provide the human dimensions to historical events. Instead, propaganda as a methodology emphasizes the *production* of a collective voice in its contentious multiplicity.

For many feminist scholars, social history gives the subaltern masses a chance to speak. In social histories, the invisible subjects of history, whether those subjects are described as peasants or non-caste Hindus, are subjects who didn't simply survive history; they lived alongside and against its dominant meanings. Feminist historians have reshaped our understanding of the past through these marginalized individual accounts of people. They have both reconstructed and dismantled dominant historical timelines of rulers and wars from the perspectives of forgotten women and men. However, as ultimately individualist methods of social rather than political history, they obscure rather than clarify consensus around emergent theories for social change. The methodologies of social history cannot describe peasant women's praxis, that is, their theories about how to struggle and what to demand. In the case of mid-twentieth-century leftist women's movements in rural centers of anticolonial movements, the erasure of collective theories of praxis at regional and national levels has global consequences. A more radical history of transnational feminism disappears—as does the leadership by peasant women at its heart.

For my own journey, social historical methods allowed some stories to emerge with greater clarity, particularly the surprisingly well-documented rural social movements peopled in large part by women, such as the Tebhaga movement for a larger portion of the crops by sharecropping farmers, a movement that erupted across Bengal, India from 1946–1948. But social historical methods also muddied the roots of a mass-based transnational feminist *theory*. These well-honed feminist methods, that gave voice to forgotten individuals and paid attention to their wider collective knowledge base, obscured rather than clarified the contours of internationalist feminist theories in the mid-twentieth century.

Pamphlets and slogans, I argue, provide more explicit keys to collective praxis. Political pamphlets are necessarily propaganda: they seek to persuade in favor of a particular understanding or course of action. Methodologically, I needed to invert standard social history methods of analysis to read propaganda as a text collectively conceived, rather than as one delivered down by a sinister force. I began with the often abstract, persuasive statements, reports and slogans as the results of hard-won theories of action. I learned to listen for contradictions and elisions, as well as consensus, in the propaganda—the underlying cacophony that signifies a range of ideas cobbled together. In this way, reading propaganda revealed more about emergent praxis developed by peasant, working-class, and middle-class leftist women activists than literate activists' diaries, and even than interviews with peasant women revolutionaries, could.

CHAPTER TWO

The Journey to the Conference

CARTOGRAPHIES OF STRUGGLE

Everybody comes from somewhere—and that place has its own cartography of struggle, bound by histories and cultures, but also by climate and soil, by mountains and rainfall. These layered conditions make their movements and temper as they nurture the span of people's movement horizons. In Asia, as the Marxist economists Utsa Patnaik and Prabhat Patnaik remind us, its climate, its geology, its fresh water sources, not to mention the breadth of its contiguous land mass and the proliferation of its islands, create its cultural wealth over time with its complex layers of human settlements and resettlements, its material wealth of resources buried under the surface, and the sheer fertility of its agricultural possibility.[1] The women who moved towards Beijing in 1949 were no different—they came from somewhere, from their own cartographies of struggle, to join with women from across the continent. Some, like Ho Thi Minh from her communist autonomous zone of northern Vietnam, began their journeys six months before the planned meeting date, walking on foot through landmines, aerial strafing, and colonial patrols. They sought to gather with their Asian sisters to make anew a world after global war, to imagine a world with no war, at the very moment they carried guns filled with live ammunition, ready for use. They left their places, the rural and urban locations of their birth as well as their uprooted locations in the colonial centers of European power. They brought with them the lessons of their struggles, some held in common with each other, some particular to their place. They gathered in Beijing with their wealth of lessons learned to bury the greed and class warfare of capitalism for good.[2]

SMOKING

Lillah Suripno boarded the Vladivostok Express in Moscow on November 23, 1949. Lillah was the only delegate from Indonesia joining the Asian Women's Conference in Beijing. Due to revolutionary upheaval in Indonesia, the women's organization Kowani had severed its relationship to the WIDF. Too dangerous, perhaps, and too contentious for the Muslim women's groups in their coalition. Since Lillah lived in Amsterdam, her working-class women's group of overseas Indonesian cooks, nannies, students, and others remained intact, however small and under close surveillance by the Dutch police. Lillah was not from a working-class background. She was educated and highly literate, but she'd worked hard to make sure she organized the working-class Indonesian women in the Netherlands. And her efforts threatened the colonial government, because the ongoing Indonesian revolution drew strength from these cross-class solidarities, even when overseas in Holland.

In Moscow, Lillah attended the Executive Committee meeting of the WIDF, and she chafed at the debate about WIDF's outreach and propaganda to women in Europe and the United States. Support for anti-colonialism was the first agenda item; everyone agreed on that. But the debates about what anti-imperialist solidarity meant in practice were more divided, The intervention by the Swedish member, Andrea Andreen, in the Budapest Congress of 1948 still drifted perceptibly in the air of the executive committee meeting a year later. Andrea had contended that WIDF's publications about anti-imperialism were too strident, with their direct focus on the United States, France, England, and the Netherlands. She suggested that WIDF's language about peace might alienate women from these imperial countries. Peace, Andrea thought, should be more even-handed as an appeal. As one example, letters calling for peace should go to all nations, including the USSR and Soviet Socialist Republics. Lillah disagreed. In her experience, soft-pedaling imperialism had never won freedom movements anything.

In Moscow, Lillah stayed close to her comrades, the Dutch communist women she knew well. When she first arrived in Amsterdam, at the age of nineteen, she had heard about their actions before she met them. Their refusal to accept colonial militarism was legendary among radical Indonesian students. At the docks of Ijmuiden on the banks of the English Channel, the women shouted "Houses not barracks!" and "Bring the troops back from Indonesia!" Their actions forced armaments back to their trucks. Alongside dockworkers, they laid their bodies across the road, forcing trucks to turn around. They kept the barges empty of bullets, machine guns, bombs, and other counterinsurgency hardware. The Dutch communist women took their blows for anti-imperialism.

In Lillah's early years, before the Nazi invasion, Dutch communists in parliament protested the brutal crackdowns in Indonesia. Colonialism was a system of wealth extraction from the colonies to the imperial centers. But Dutch communists spread another lesson among the working classes: all workers were exploited for their labor. In the capitalist system, Indonesian workers and Dutch workers were pitted against each other—separated by oceans, by differential treatment, by a system of unequal competition for survival. These communists said things out loud, in public places, about capitalism and about colonialism that weren't allowed to be whispered in Palembang, Lillah's hometown in Sumatra, Indonesia. Lillah witnessed how the veneer of democratic civilization was maintained only for the citizens of Holland, who could debate colonialism publicly. That civilizational mission was not honored where she was born, colonial subjects did not need to be convinced of the rightness of colonialism, they merely had to submit. Those harsh truths of the ruling order didn't soften the radicalism of Dutch communists' fight for the international unity of workers against the old capitalist tactic of divide and rule. They insisted that until everyone was free, no one was free.

Lillah had grown up in a doctor's household. Her father, Raden Soesilo, was the acting head of the Malaria Control Division of the Dutch East Indies Public Health Service. Lillah, her mother Nyonya, and her brother Brenthel came to Amsterdam together so her father could continue his medical education. Her father returned to Indonesia alone, however, with his superior medical knowledge. He became the resident doctor of Banjarmasin before the Japanese forces occupied Indonesia in 1941. Lillah remained in Amsterdam, living in their house at Euterpestraat 167 with her mother and Brenthel. Together, they waited for her brother to complete his studies in economics in Rotterdam before they rejoined their father. But those plans changed. Lillah would never return to Indonesia again, not even to bury her husband after he was executed.[3]

When Lillah boarded the Trans-Siberian train to Beijing, she joined her Amsterdam comrades, Hanna Averink and Rie Lips-Odinot, in their second-class compartment. She appreciated the first, and she loved the second. Hanna skated on the thin ice of resistance throughout the war, never leaving the front lines of its struggle, brushing away from numerous close shaves with the dexterity of a skater. Trained in Moscow during the 1930s, some said in spycraft, Hanna stayed lucky. Rie had spent most of the war as a political prisoner in the Ravensbruck concentration camp, but everyone knew her easy laugh and the energetic lift of her arms when she spoke, the curl of her lip when she listened. All this drew Lillah to her in the years before her arrest. They grew closer after both were released from imprisonment in 1945.

During the 1930s, Lillah joined the Perhimpunan Indonesia, simply called PI, a nationalist organization very close to the communists, alongside the other Indonesian students, most of whom did not come from professional families like hers. Most were noble, or rich, or both. They had lavish parties. They threw spectacular, nostalgic cultural events to celebrate where they came from. So, even before the Nazis invaded the Netherlands, Lillah joined the Dutch anti-fascist resistance. She knew everyone by then, she trusted them enough to risk her life every day, even when betrayal sent her closest friends to the concentration camps. She and her brother Brenthel joined the resistance secure, safe even, in the knowledge of why they joined: to fight the fascist invasion. They aided the underground movement of people, of Dutch Jews mostly, but also German emigres who flooded into the country. They found hiding places in the forest of Veluwe for two groups of Jewish children so they could survive the terrible occupation, the soldiers, the barbed wire, and on-the-ready weaponry alive.[4]

She and her brother fought a fascism they knew only too well in Indonesia, one that enforced illiteracy on the vast masses of people it said were theirs to rule. A fascism that stole every resource hidden in the ground for its industries, its profits. A fascism that forced children to work for six to seven hours a day when small and eleven to twelve hours a day by the time they were ten. Their own lives were privileged in Indonesia, but the malaria patients treated by her father day in and day out told another story. They lived lives under the crushing heel of fascism in the colonies. Lillah also became a communist during this period. She proudly became someone who said the unthinkable aloud, and attended the clandestine resistance meetings held in her house. She worked in her home's attic alongside her comrades to publish resistance newspapers and flyers on the stencil machine hidden there, churning out forbidden news for distribution to the population. The Nazis never discovered the stencil in the attic, even though it cranked out anti-fascist propaganda in the same neighborhood as the headquarters of the Sicherheitsdienst, the Germans' infamous security services.

In their train compartment on the Vladivostok Express, there were only a couple of hooks, so Lillah, Hanna, and Rie kept their clothes packed in their suitcases tucked under the bottom berth. The train was too cold to take off their coats much anyway, and spare hooks were not the issue in the end. They settled themselves for a long journey. Some played dominoes and other games to pass the time. Like everyone going to the conference, they talked with each other and shared explanations of their lives and struggles with the other second-class compartment delegates traveling to the Asian Women's Conference.

Two conversations among many: Gisele Rabesahala from Madagascar packed a cabin one evening with her stories of their struggles against the French. Gisele could hold her own in any space: she was a founder of the communist Congress Party for the Independence of Madagascar. Two years earlier she led the Malagasy Solidarity Committee to demand the release of ninety thousand political prisoners who had been accused of leading a rebellion against the French occupation. She described the old colonial tactics of warfare, pitting Senegalese and Sudanese soldiers against them, since according to French colonial logics, "you can't trust the Madagascar soldiers to subdue their own."[5] But divide and conquer was powerful within the country as well, she said: those who lived on the plateau of the island were pitted against the people of the lowlands, by the French and the powerful. Even nationalism on the island, that sense of unity within a country of different religions, cultures, and dialects, had to be created as a whole cloth. She described how after the war ended in Europe, French terror in Madagascar had only increased, and now she was forced to live and organize wholly underground.

Ding Ling, the famous Chinese author, described the revolutionary tactics that had won over the Chinese masses, overwhelmingly farmers. "Rely on the poor peasants; Unite with the middle peasants; Isolate the rich peasants; Fight the landlords."[6] She had worked in the liberated areas for many years, and land reform was first, with land titles given to landless women as well as men. But even before, she said, "we Communists had to make lower rent, lower taxes, and land reform.... [S]eventy five percent of the peasants' income went to landlords. Tenants had to provide fertilizer, seeds, labor; landlords only provided land. At harvest time tenants must give half and best of their crop to the landlord. When peasants can't pay, they go into debt at enormous interest rates which accumulate more debt."[7] Alongside land reform, their Chinese cadre fought for universal education for girls and boys, men and women, and for local systems of representation with universal rights to vote.

The delegates from Lebanon and Syria, Salma Boummi, Amine Araf Hasan, and Victoria Helou were close, like Lillah was with Hanna and Rie. Like her circle, they came from Muslim and Christian religious cultures, but shared a passion for women's rights and a hatred of colonial occupation. But they all had children, families, and lives rich beyond their activism alone. Mahine Faroqi, from Iran, was young like Lillah, and she also had no children. The communist Tudeh Party in Iran was underground again, banned by the Shah's regime. Only a year before, Iran's most well-known activist for women's liberation, Maryam Firouz, had joined WIDF's Congress of Women in Budapest with her fiery speeches and sharp demands for anti-imperialist solidarity from the American delegates in particular. In the words of Firouz: "Let the American people know that their representatives order mass imprisonment, massacres and tortures. Tell your people that, supported and strengthened by American imperialism, the reactionaries in Iran crushed the young peoples' movement of Azerbaijan."[8] Her notoriety to the Shah's government meant leaving the country was out of the question in 1949. Mahine Faroqi was young, less well-known to the police than Firouz, and managed to gain a visa to travel to Moscow. Unlike Lillah, she hadn't yet lost a lover, a husband, a fiancé, someone daring, audacious and unquenchable, to a pragmatic execution, a single bullet to his head for his dedicated service to his republic.

Lillah's fiancé, known by his last name Suripno, studied chemistry at the University of Leiden and was on the front lines of every daring action by the PI. He was charismatic, always laughing, and fiercely arguing. He never eased the lines of his demands for Indonesian independence, refusing to be compromised by a Dutch commonwealth status, or by Dutch capital knotting the economy on apron strings of everlasting debt and dependence. Suripno was from an aristocratic family, and he led the PI after their leader Kurtosudirdjo was arrested by the Germans in 1941 and died in Dachau a year later. Suripno edited *De Beurijding* (The Liberator), published three times a week with a print run of 20,000 copies by the end of the war. Suripno also founded "Surapati," a domestic armed contingent that trained in Leiden.[9] They led military actions against the Nazis, stealing and stockpiling their weapons to use later to kill German officers. His courage never seemed to flag. Lillah, too, took chances; everyone did.

She dared to live aloud during the occupation. The careful secrets of writing, stenciling, printing, and distributing resistance publications filled her nights. After the schools were shut down, her days were just as busy with her friends in PI, her comrades across color lines, across colonial lines. She took a chance in the public limelight in August 1943. The dance that she organized to raise funds for the resistance movement was elaborate, beautifully staged, held in the soaring proscenium theater the Schouwburg in Amsterdam. Despite the constant surveillance and harassment of Nazi occupation, all the Indonesian students who had not yet been imprisoned took a chance for the resistance, for beauty. Only weeks before the performance, the PI secretary was roused from his bed and dragged to a prison cell. Like the previous PI secretary, Kurtosudirdjo, he died in Dachau. Still, Lillah danced for

Figure 3. Lillah Soesilo (Suripno), performing in "Tangkuban Prahoe" ("Upturned Boat"), Amsterdam, Holland, August 1943. Photo courtesy of Harry Poeze.

three performances in "Tangkuban Prahoe" ("Upturned Boat"), a Sundanese legend, with live gamelan music and a *dalang*-narrator, present in her body, present in her past.

A photograph shows her in this performance of "Tangkuban Prahoe."[10] Her body is lit from the side, casting a shadow behind her reclining form. Her shoulders are bare, vulnerable. She gazes reflectively down at the shape of an overturned boat hull with a painted backdrop of dense forest leaves. These cultural performances were political too. The money raised from ticket sales funded the anti-fascist resistance movement. Her calm, relaxed posture in the photograph shows how she enacted the role of Dayan Sumbi, the ill-fated princess, but also how she portrayed another role: that of a simple cultural ambassador in a colonial capital occupied by fascist troops.

She never regretted her daring, not later, not after. She remained a communist. Days after her successful performance, she learned of her father's public beheading by Japanese forces occupying Indonesia—a warning for the entire island against any disobedience. A comrade in the resistance gleaned the information from a late-night broadcast, news stolen from radio waves forbidden by the Nazis. Even her father, the very doctor trained at the world's finest medical facilities who could alleviate the malaria that decimated fascist troops, could not be spared Japanese retribution. His nationalism was a threat more important than his knowledge of how to heal. When his head was severed from his body, they sought to remove his brain from his actions, his ideals from their purpose.

Before she learned of her father's murder, she had been able to dance and to act. She could project the mother's/lover's regret and sadness of the mythic princess Dayan Sumbi, and the innocent grace of an Indonesian performer sharing her cultural stories far from home. Within days of this performance and just after she learned about her father's violent death, the Gestapo came for her and her brother Brenthel. She arrived in the Dutch concentration camp Vught, and was charged with aiding the underground movement. Those charges left out her many crimes in the eyes of fascists: her communism and her anti-imperialism, her fervor as a saboteur, anti-fascist propagandist, protector of Jewish people, daughter of nationalists, and dancer for the people. She survived. And they failed to subdue her commitments, especially now when she had so little to lose.

On the Trans-Siberian Railway, smoking was not a convenient habit. Crossing the Ural mountains in the dead of night was cold. The windows of the train constantly fogged with droplets of moisture congealing to slip down the grimy windowpanes.

Women opened and shut the doors to their compartments quickly to keep their warm breath and body heat from escaping. In the Mongolian steppes, colder still, smoking became a kind of punishment. Perhaps due to the frigid conditions, the three French leaders of WIDF rarely left their first-class compartments to walk back to the second-class compartments and mingle. Neither did their fourth companion in first class, Anezka Hodinova, a parliament member from Czechoslovakia, who said little, hunched over her notebooks during the day, wrapped in blankets.

One argument unfolded over several days of the journey, between two WIDF members who lived in the central offices of Paris. Jeannette Vermeersch was a member of the French parliament, the French Assembly, and a powerful member of the French Communist Party. Betty Millard was an American member of the Communist Party, and she had been working in Paris, coordinating activities, replying to international members' mail, and editing the WIDF's publications. She mentioned the solitary, closed-off lives of the WIDF leaders in their first-class quarters. Jeannette came back to their quarters on the fourth day of the journey, perhaps in response to her criticism. But she didn't answer it directly. "Smoking is a betrayal of the working class," Jeannette Vermeersch declared on that fourth day.[11] She settled into the compartment like a rebuke, and listed the reasons as if through the curling smoke from Betty's cigarette.

Others pushed into the cabin to listen and share their opinions. Lillah may have watched Betty's cool gaze grow flinty, hardened by the Frenchwoman's arguments. Betty was also living in Paris; she worked with Jeannette at the same central offices of WIDF, writing and translating. Betty didn't seem to mind in the least being in second class, sharing her compartment with Baya Allaouchiche from Algeria and the two comrades from Mongolia, Jsivigruydin Dulmavshav and Tamara Khanum. If Baya or Tamara didn't like the smoke, Betty would have slipped out into the frigid corridors to enjoy her cigarettes, probably wearing her ankle-length fur coat with aplomb, gazing into the thickly frosted windows as she exhaled.

In Moscow, Betty's attitude, her friendly American certitude, did not make Betty and Lillah friends. Betty's laugh came quickly, as so many photographs from this period record. But her journals show that this humor usually had more than a hint of sardonic distance; humor could act as an armor against the conversations that made her uncomfortable. And Lillah made her uncomfortable, as demonstrated by more than one line in Betty's journal. Betty wrote of Lillah's "histrionics" and her "competition with the train whistles" on their journey.[12] For Lillah, imperialism, not just anti-colonialism, was the point. Comfortable invocations of solidarity with Asian women fighting the beheading of their loved ones, and the summary murder of their comrade-husbands, was weak comfort. Solidarity in practice was more difficult than vague feelings of empathy or regret.

Imperialism was for Betty to carry—North American capital, North American weaponry, North American military bases, North American profits, North American consumption of all of Lillah's country's resources. The United States, the new imperialist boss of the globe, bankrolled her country's embattlement at the hands of the Dutch and their Indonesian puppet leaders. Brenthal, her own brother who fought alongside her in the resistance movement, thought the Americans had liberated him from the concentration camp, an error that severed their easy love for each other. Her brother joined the Indonesian army immediately after the war ended. He quickly rose to become the head of intelligence in Yogyakarta, collaborating with the first CIA agent sent to Indonesia, Arturo Campbell.[13]

Essie Robeson and Ada Jackson, both well-known activists in anti-racist movements from America, were also on the train. They grasped the necessary depth of solidarities. Essie had a husband, Paul Robeson, who was both as famous (and, in anti-communist circles, infamous) in her country as Lillah's husband was in hers. Essie repeated the Asian women's slogan in her diaries of the conference as well as her journalistic articles after it ended. "Colonialism is dead, all that remains is for us to bury the corpse."[14] Perhaps Lillah could imagine digging that grave alongside Essie, both of them powered by an undercurrent of rage at the racialism of fascism at home and imperialism abroad, a rage that woke with the morning and barely slept at night.

But Betty of the agile pen, of constant language lessons in Russian with the journalist Olga Milosevic, of conversations with everyone on the train, flitted through the compartments as if by gesture and games alone. Her easy charm was a stark contrast with Lillah's intensity of purpose. When Jeannette began to lecture Betty on her smoking, Lillah may have settled in for the show at first. Jeannette elaborated: Smoking was okay for men, but not for women. It was simply not feminine. Olga, perhaps not fully realizing the stakes of this onslaught, agreed with Jeannette: it was okay for women like Betty who had no children, but not for mothers. Olga and her comrade Nadezhda Parfenova also had second-class cabins and spent the endless hours in conversations, relaxing while they could. Jeannette may have seen her opening then; she knew Olga and Betty were friendly. Jeannette continued. Not only was smoking unfeminine, it betrayed an envy for men, an aping of their bad habits; the cigarette was a symbolic way to gain the upper hand, if only subconsciously.

Then it was Nadezhda who failed to take the edge off the argument. She remarked that in the Soviet Union only women who worked "in the apparatus," that is, in the bureau offices, smoked. Working-class women, she said, didn't have the time. Jeannette offered one more parting shot: "It is strange that Casanova had such a happy life given how much he smoked. His wife loved him." Betty fell silent, it seems, since her journal mentions no witty rejoinder. Later, Olga told her to fight back harder. Jeannette was, as Betty noted in French in her journal, "une donne des eclairsoisements et des armament," that is, "a woman of clarity and weapons."[15] Did Jeannette's last comment insinuate that Casanova, the legendary womanizer, might be the person Betty sought to copy but could never achieve? Betty's sexual attraction for women may have been known to those, like Jeannette, staffing the Paris offices of the WIDF. Later, in her memoirs, she wrote about her time in Paris as the turning point when she took comfort, joy even, in the sheer possibility of her erotic love for women. In Paris, she wrote, women's sexual lives with other women were just part of the accepted social fabric of life. In the train, to break the awkward silence, Olga changed the subject and told her own story: of her father's murder during the Russian civil war when she was young. She described her job in a tobacco factory as a small girl, and the merciful support of the Young Communist League who raised the funds so she could quit working for a few years and get an education. Olga was a journalist of good standing because of the communists' commitment to her potential as a waif of a girl.

Even the next day, Betty's criticism of the WIDF leaders' standoffishness, its whiff of class privilege, must have stung Jeannette. She returned again to the second-class compartments with six thoughts about smoking, some of them repetitive. Smoking is revolting. Smoking is an imitation of men to feel strong.

Thoughts three and four: smoking is a crutch. Fifth, smoking is an attempt to distance oneself when working—an act of "navel gazing, tree-sitting dream world that avoided struggle," to be exact.[16] Her sixth thought offered a surprising caveat: after dinner, smoking was okay, like drinking a postprandial coffee.

Jeannette's argument about smoking as a betrayal of the working classes seemed to stand in for something else. Betty's observation of a leadership that failed to mix with the larger delegation of women on a long, cold train journey was barbed, but did not rise to a betrayal of shared ideals. For Lillah, these arguments would have been trivial. As her speeches revealed at the conference, she had more elemental disagreements with her comrades about the need for absolute militance in the destruction of imperialism. The one-year anniversary of Suripno's execution for sedition was two weeks away: on December 19, 1948 he had been killed with a single bullet by Indonesia's Hatta government. For all she knew, her powerful brother had supplied the surveillance information that killed her husband. Imperialism had intervened to cut short the Indonesian people's revolution, one fought and died for by the working classes and peasants, more by them than by middle-class people like herself or royal elites like her husband. The enemy was clear as the day itself, and she fought for a movement daring enough to eradicate it.

Lillah had married Suripno as soon as the war ended in Europe. Eager to join the Indonesian independence movement, Suripno led the Indonesian students' delegation at the World Federation of Democratic Youth in London in 1945. Afterwards he returned to Indonesia to join the front lines of the independence struggle. When asked by Sjarifuddin, the prime minister of independent Indonesia, he flew to Prague in 1948 as the Indonesian representative of the International Union of Students, where it was headquartered.[17] Sjarifuddin also designated him to act as the ambassador plenipotentiary to begin delicate negotiations with the USSR for recognition of the Indonesian Republic. The new republic was on shaky ground internationally, with its legitimacy unrecognized by the major powers of Europe and the United States. When the Renville talks with the Netherlands were signed, an uneasy truce prevailed. As the negotiations dragged on, the Americans, who had promised neutrality as the third party in the talks, blatantly took the side of the Dutch.[18] The US politicians did nothing when the Dutch launched an economic blockade of the Indonesian Republic in Java, starving the island of resources by allowing nothing in and nothing out. They looked the other way while the Dutch violated their own agreement and sought to economically strangle the independent Republic. Unsurprisingly, in this context, the sticking point of the negotiations was economic. The Dutch refused all compromise on the bottom line of colonialism: the right to own and control Indonesia's means of production. And they demanded the transfer of all capital debt in the country to the Indonesians, even while foreign corporations housed in the Netherlands drained away the profits from these same industries. The one victory of these talks sat cold and hard in the stomach: the Dutch agreed that the Indonesians would be allowed to use that word to describe themselves, instead of the Dutch colonial term "native."[19] Dutch greed trumped their invocations of European supremacy.

The United Nations ignored Indonesians' appeals for justice in the face of Dutch intransigence. All the western European countries refused to recognize the Indonesian Republic. Suripno flew to Prague to negotiate international recognition by the USSR. He succeeded, but when the Russians announced their decision, the Hatta government refused the diplomatic hand extended by the Soviet Union—they were in too deep with the US government to accept it. Suripno was recalled to Indonesia, and the gesture of international recognition from the USSR became his shame, the noose around his neck.

And then the story got messy—a union fight erupted in the city of Madiun, in September 1948, far from the capital. The labor struggle escalated into a battle between the leftist nationalist groups and the more conservative Hatta government. Hatta's government imprisoned thirty-five thousand people as a result, including Suripno. But fighting two fronts at once, Indonesian leftists and Dutch colonists, was impossible. The Dutch broke the Renville agreement and militarily attacked Yogyakarta to arrest the leaders of the Indonesian Republic, an act that tipped the balance of power. The Hatta government could not alienate Indonesian nationalists while under attack from the Dutch military forces. Hatta needed these nationalist prisoners on his side, on the Indonesian government's side. So, in the interests of the Republic, all thirty-five thousand of the workers, labor leaders, and leftists were freed, with eleven exceptions. Eleven leaders of the leftist faction were shot by Hatta's government on December 19, 1948, and Suripno was one of them.[20]

For Lillah, and those in the Communist Party of Indonesia (PKI), Suripno fought for an independence that struck at the heart of capitalism. The PKI and their coalition allies saw the economic deceit in the negotiations between Hatta's government and the Dutch government, a deception actively abetted by their interlocutors, representing the United States. By 1950, that deceit became the price of independence, a price that handed over all of the weapons of financial capitalism, including Indonesia's banks, its powerful firms, and swaths of valuable land to the Dutch. Independence with economic dependence. In 1950, Indonesia was free: free to starve at the hands of Dutch banks and Dutch corporations. In Marxist terms, the Dutch still hoarded the means of production and could turn the financial screws on the Indonesian economy by controlling money supply and draining the nation's surplus value into Dutch coffers. Betty Millard could voice her solidarity with Indonesian women fighting for independence, but have little idea of what it should mean for her, or the role her government played in Lillah's movement. Lillah's "steam whistle" of anger, in Betty's words, can also be understood as the force required to pry Americans from their innocence.

After Jeannette's victory on the gender, sexuality, and class politics of smoking, she came to the second-class coaches more often, with more of her opinions about the world. Unequivocally, she stated, "the French working class is not racist."[21] And even though Betty and Lillah crossed swords in Moscow over American imperialism and meaningful anti-colonial solidarity, Lillah told Betty what she thought about the smoking debate on the train. "Isn't it interesting," Lillah said, facing Betty's wary gaze as they returned to their train in Shenyang, China, only one more stop in Tianjin away from Beijing.[22] "Some people don't smoke because they want to be closer to the working class. Meanwhile, they take no great personal interest in other problems."[23] Lillah's inference was clear: Jeannette saw no need to address endemic working-class European racism, as natural as a coffee, or a cigarette, after dinner. She refused to see the possibility of her own hierarchal instincts or to admit to the difficulties of building an international workers' solidarity across the very real barriers of colonial, racist conceptions of hierarchy and difference. I imagine that Lillah saw Betty's face relax at that moment and a hint of a smile cross her eyes. "She has a point," Betty wrote in her journal that evening.

TRAVEL BY FOOT, AND THOSE WHO STAYED HOME

Not everyone traveled to the conference by train or plane.[24] Some of the delegates from South and Southeast Asia walked. To reach the gathering of leftist women, they crossed armed Asian borders patrolled by colonial soldiers from Nepal, Algeria, Morocco, and Senegal, all soldiers hired or conscripted by the Dutch, British, and French, soldiers who were shipped around the world as their employers saw fit. Three delegations of women traveled to China with no passports and no visas, no signatures or official stamps from embassies. These groups of women were militants, from the countries then called Burma (Myanmar), Malaya (Malaysia), and North Vietnam (Vietnam). Each walked through active war zones to reach the Asian women's conference in Beijing. All of these delegations came from struggles that could not be won easily or quickly. They could not be won without solidarity among the comrades who shared their Asian aspirations for freedom. Each of these delegations had woman who made it on time, but their journeys were long, dangerous, and they left people behind.

Ho Thi Minh left three months earlier than her five other comrades chosen as delegates, since she had planned to help with preparations for the conference in China. In the end, the journey took six months, and she was the only delegate who arrived in time.[25] She began her journey in the liberated zone of the northern highlands of Vietnam, navigating the paths she'd walked most of her life. In North Vietnam, her cadre in the National Liberation Front were settling in for a long fight. The French forces, gathered from colonies around the world, had increased in the southern parts of Vietnam, preparing to assault the hard-won independence of the Vietnamese. The small skirmishes, fought with devastating but inaccurate bombs from overhead, had failed in their mission: to frighten them into submission, into dropping their mantle of a free republic, to agreeing to return to France's colonial fold, docile as newly tamed sheep. These bombs targeted schools and homes as much as they destroyed bridges or roads or Vietnamese military posts. And the soldiers on the ground had a similar task: whole villages murdered for no reason at all, not even a question unanswered. And these slaughters came after each and every woman, crone and girl child had been raped, sexually assaulted with rifles and sticks and bottles.[26] Their bodies, bayoneted and dismembered, were not burned in their houses, but left behind as warnings to residents of surrounding hamlets. Grow your rice, they said, if corpses could speak. Keep your head down, they moaned. Pay your taxes, read the palms of outstretched hands melting in the new summer rains.

Twice, Ho Thi Minh evaded French military cordons to reach Vietnamese shores, attempting to take a boat up the coastline to China. Both times she was arrested, detained, and turned back. The third time she tried another route: this time, she took a ship to France. From France she took another ship to China. It took her six months, but she reached Beijing in time to dance with Zhou Enlai, the Premier of China, on the first night of the conference, although too late to help, as planned, with the conference preparations.

Ongoing colonial assaults rejected their declarations of Asian independence, so Ho Thi Minh and her comrades put down their weapons, took time off from vital work to support the armed resistance, to join the Asian Women's Conference with its speeches, parties, and resolutions. They sought to build a regional solidarity with revolutionary women from around the world in New China, one finally led by the Communist Party of China. They sought recognition of their countries' embattled independence, one that in the eyes of imperialist nations should have been short-lived and easily forgotten. In 1948, at WIDF's Second Congress, Vietnamese delegate Pham Ngoc Thuan described the high stakes of the Asian Women's Conference beyond diplomatic international recognition. "We strongly hope that the exchange of views between the delegates of the different countries of Asia, the experiences of the peoples in their struggles will help the Congress to work out resolutions which will ensure energetic support to the resistance movement of the women of Asia."[27]

Ling Lang walked and then took a ship from Malaya. As in Vietnam, the safest areas of the country were the most remote, those deepest in mountainous terrain. Her comrades were peasants and plantation workers—some were Malay, but most were of Indian or Chinese origin, transported by British colonists to ensure divisions in the ranks of rubber and other plantation workers. These comrades kept her safe, even when nothing was safe. Ling Lang successfully joined the conference and gave her address to her comrades. Ting Thien Gui walked from Myanmar, a country torn by a civil war after the bad-faith independence promised by the British in 1946. They called it independence, but the region was still locked into the finances of long-distance colonialism: British corporations still siphoned out all of the profits of their industry, of their mining, of their rubber plantations. Puppet governments in Vietnam, Malaya, and Burma relied on colonial financing and American weaponry to stay in power. The peoples' resistance to this new colonialism-by-proxy produced what they called a civil war—

but these were civil wars with colonial troops, imperialist bombs, and capitalist planes that dropped those bombs. Ting Thien Gui didn't start out alone, but her companion, another woman from her movement, was shot by a British soldier and had to turn back.[28]

Other women from other countries were barred from attending. Charlotta Bass, an African American civil rights activist and journalist, was denied a passport by the US government. Wei The, the overseas Chinese delegate from Thailand, described similar intransigence: "three more delegates who have prepared to attend this momentous conference, but owing to the various obstructions by the Songgram reactionary government (in Thailand), they have been delayed and are still on the way, unable to attend the Conference."[29] The only delegate from the Philippines had been living in China for decades. In 1948, the US-backed government had crushed the communist and workers' struggle of the Hukbalahap Rebellion on the island of Luzon. The US had also made sure their grip around Filipinos' travel to and from the islands was tightened so no dissidents to American-backed rule left or entered the country. For the Japanese delegation, only Tanaga Hamaku, a Japanese revolutionary woman living in China, could attend. She represented the large delegation from Japan who were forbidden to attend the conference by MacArthur's occupying government in Japan. Scholar Mire Koikari describes the letters between Song Qingling, an important, if largely symbolic leader in the All-China Democratic Women's Federation and Miyamoto Yuriko, the leader of the Japan Democratic Women's Council.[30] In protest of their visa denials, the Japanese activists held a parallel Asian Women's Conference in Tokyo on December 16 and 17, 1949. Song's letters to Miyamoto described the conference in Beijing in ebullient terms. "All shared the will to oppose imperialist wars, bring eternal peace to the world, and emancipate colonized populations."[31]

These women shared movements that did not regard women's emancipation as secondary to national liberation. As communist independence movements, they sought emancipation for all: peasants, workers, women, multiethnic, multireligious, and indigenous peoples. They recognized the differences among these forms of human relations; all saw the need for women's organizations, even as they had youth groups, peasant unions, and workers' unions. The world they wanted to build was larger than one nation, and included all working class and peasant people left behind in capitalism. In Ho Thi Minh's report to the Asian Women's Conference, she demanded a more resolute, a fiercer solidarity from the French women who vowed that women's rights were only possible in a just world. She greeted the conference on its first day: "Coming directly from the resistance movement in Viet Nam, I am happy to extend to you the greetings and the solidarity in struggle of the women of Viet Nam, united in the ranks of the Union of Vietnamese Women."[32] As Vietnam's liberation leader Ho Chi Minh famously said: women make up half of society. If they are not liberated, half of society is not freed. If women are not emancipated, socialism cannot be built.

When they arrived in Beijing, the new capital of the People's Republic of China, the air was cold. Delegates stayed bundled up at their seats in the Winter Palace. Banners hung on the walls of the main meeting hall, named "A Place Where We Think About Humanity," celebrated this historic gathering of anti-imperialist women activists. Women from Vietnam, Indonesia, Myanmar, and Malaysia described the colonial wars that buried women's rights under the rubble of warfare. As their crops were burned, bridges bombed, and roads laid waste under the onslaught, the Asian Women's Conference imagined women's rights in independent nations *as peace* even while they fought for that vision through military warfare. The Asian Women's Conference did not ignore the rest of the world to support Asia's needs; instead, it sought an internationalism among women that was strong enough to survive colonial re-enslavement and imperialism everywhere. The Asian Women's Conference sought women's equal legal rights to education, to marital and divorce rights, equal pay for equal work, an end to violence and polygamy, state support for childcare, and to property rights. They held these goals in common with all people seeking women's emancipation. Simply, the conference sought a just peace framed by women's economic, political and cultural rights. Ling Lang, Ting Thien Gui, and Ho Thi Minh walked all those miles to the conference in Beijing. Each footstep measured the distance they'd come and the aspirations that fueled them, as representatives of the thousands of women who peopled their struggles. When they arrived, they took their experiences from the struggle to collectively create a theory for women's internationalism that would guide the praxis of anti-imperialist women who spanned the globe.

CHAPTER THREE

An Anatomy of Revolutionary Women's Praxis

The Asian Women's Conference was a massive undertaking for a new socialist country. It opened on December 10, 1949 and lasted for seven days. Delegates listened to speeches and country reports as well as attended ceremonies and performances. The conference was held in the elaborate Winter Palace of the Forbidden City, whose art and architecture were once only accessible to the elite and their servants. Cultural innovation was a vital part of the Chinese Communist Party's revolution. The Asian Women's Conference showcased an incredible range of artistic experiments in theater, dance, song and film. At a dinner hosted by Zhou Enlai, the Chinese premier, conference delegates listened to Chinese jazz and danced the lindy hop. Yu Xixuan, a famous soprano who had been featured in the film *Spring in a Small Town* (1948), gave a talk about Chinese revolutionary music. She described experiments with tone, harmony, instrumentation, and voice range that drew upon both the folk music of Chinese ethnic minorities and western music.[1] Chen Bo'er, the revolutionary filmmaker, would later dedicate her film

Daughters of China to the Asian Women's Conference.² Outside the conference room, the All-China Democratic Women's Federation set up book tables and the National Art Academy exhibited work by revolutionary artists, mostly brightly colored *nianhua* drawings from the revolutionary Yan'an arts movement, that celebrated the victories of rural women under socialism: land rights, voting, holding elected offices, and education. One drawing portrayed rural land reform and women's new right to hold property; the text read, "We have our land certificates—we must increase production. Better days are coming!"³

"Many delegates from the Asiatic countries have risked their lives to come to the Conference, crossing firing lines and outwitting the watchfulness of secret agents and detectives to arrive at their destination," declared Cai Chang, the vice president of WIDF and a Chinese Communist Party member since 1923, as she opened the proceedings.⁴ Translators moved among delegates to facilitate conversations and translate the speeches into Chinese, French, English, and Russian. Four languages were not sufficient; delegates came from fourteen Asian countries (Burma, China, India, Indonesia, Iran, Israel, Korea, Lebanon, Malaysia, Mongolia, the Philippines, Syria, and Vietnam).⁵

These women who had walked out of battlefields, or flown, or taken the train to gather in Beijing and share what they knew, created a theory for socialism in a capitalist world. They sat, they talked, they listened and analyzed the militant activism of women in all their differences and their commonalties to develop their praxis for women's internationalism. Delegate after delegate described the horrendous conditions faced by women, children, and men under Dutch, French, and British rule in Asian and African colonies. They spoke of planned starvation, forced labor, and conscription into colonial armies. They condemned the military occupations that gave the lie to the Western rhetoric of democracy, let alone freedom. They built the sinews of a mass-based transnational women's movement: one that fought systems of colonialism, fascism, racism, and patriarchy simultaneously.

Delegates attending the AWC lauded the bravery of peasant women as the militant backbone to both their anti-colonial struggles for independence and women's emancipation from oppressive customs. These rural women primarily fought battles against feudal landowners and old forms of subjugation based on land ownership, customary rule, and local hierarchies. And delegates agreed, capitalism had absorbed and fed upon the feudal traditions such as those around gender and caste, to extract greater profits and stabilize it. Demolishing those feudal practices that bound women to servitude and harnessed them to plows attacked capitalism as a result. There was no first or last in fighting for women's emancipation, they agreed. Fighting for all women, not just the privileged few, undermined the reproduction of capitalism itself.

For most of the Asian delegates—particularly those from Vietnam, Indonesia, Malaysia, Myanmar, Korea—and notably for the Japanese delegation barred from attending the conference, women's work in their revolutions was clandestine and life-threatening. Asian and African women aspired to women's rights to own property and their right to divorce at will. However, for many under siege, the conditions of colonialism first demanded a government that affirmed their rights to exist, to have a voice, and above all to self-determination. Ho Thi Minh provided a detailed report about Vietnamese women's roles on the frontlines of anticolonial insurgency:

> At the front, women are part of the guerilla units and the partisan detachments. The four units of women which are best known are the *Minh Khai, Trung Trao, Ma Ling* and *Hoa Dinh.*

The *Minh Khai* unit was formed at the beginning of the resistance and has co-operated with the national guards in many battles, as well as in the attack on the Kien An outpost. The *Trung Trac* unit has responsibility for all army propaganda. The *Ma Ling* unit engaged in two battles on August 1947 on Route 5, destroying four jeeps and killing twenty-four enemy soldiers. In January 1948, the *Hoa Binh* unit, using hand grenades, wiped out a group of French soldiers who were plundering and burning a village located a few kilometers from the unit's camp. The women have distinguished themselves in the scouting, liaison work and army propaganda. They manage to make their way even inside enemy-occupied territory and distribute leaflets there for the information of the population.[6]

Women were members of guerilla units and detachments, spread information about the army, scouted and spoke with the public about their war for independence. Ho Thi Minh carried another report—propaganda, to use her word—about women's emancipation in a war zone. Even in battle, women forged new gender relationships by dismantling old feudal gender expectations. The Constitution for the Democratic Republic of Vietnam of 1946 guaranteed by law the full equal rights of women and men. But it was rural farmers in small localities who took the lead in weaving these promises into daily practices. "Women share in the redistribution of land which once belonged to the traitors and the French colonizers, and the rice fields which had remained unworked during French occupation.... Each region now has its maternity hospital and clinic. Sanitary committees travel about and reach the most isolated spots to bring help to mothers in confinement. Recent figures show that infant mortality and deaths among mothers in childbirth have considerably diminished."[7] The socialist insurgency against French colonial power was not solely a war against occupation, but also sought to create a new realm for lived equality.

AWC delegates from across Asia spoke about how anticolonialism and women's full autonomy were entwined struggles. Neither national nor social self-determination could precede the other, since both were deeply embedded economic forms of enslavement to another's gain. Colonial regimes relied on localized patriarchal relationships to secure their regional control. The demand for women's self-determination was an inseparable and mutually reinforcing struggle for regional independence. For anticolonialism to have any purchase on the future, women's full emancipation was today's work, not tomorrow's aspiration. As ceremony, the Asian Women's Conference symbolized the truth of postwar imperialism: colonialism was over and revolutionary women had dug that grave. As politics, the conference evoked another future: of equality, of independence, of emancipation for all—patriarchy, fascism, racism, and imperialism would not be tolerated any longer. Colonialism, configured as the past, and socialism, hailed as the future, reverberated throughout the delegates' speeches. The most concrete gain from the gathering was one of strategy for a feminist anti-colonialism that encompassed the aspirations of women from around the globe.

WOMEN'S INTERNATIONALIST PRAXIS

The Asian Women's Conference culminated in two appeals. Both were crafted by a movement that was peopled by rural farmers fighting guerrilla wars against wealthy, powerful forces armed to the teeth. They sought to mobilize the differential relations of solidarity to show what an internationalist resistance to colonial aggression meant. Their appeal to Asian women connected their participation in anti-colonial resistance as the *means* to support their demands for full rights:

Women of the countries of Asia! Workers, peasants, white-collar workers, intellectuals—remember that in unity lies our strength and the guarantee of victory over imperialism and feudal reaction! ... Sisters, suffering under the burden of imperialism and the yoke of reaction! Unite, and in uniting, take into consideration the concrete conditions prevailing in our respective countries and adapt to them all available forms of struggle.

Women militants! Take part in all the organizations comprising masses of women, help to educate them and to defend their basic rights![8]

Their appeal provided focused left-feminist demands: for economic, political, and social rights for women. These were demands for women's education, their right to own land, and political equality—all embedded in their revolutionary mass organizational work in the countryside, towns, and cities. They were not discrete legal demands lodged with the colonial state, since dismantling regional customs (or "concrete conditions") demanded more focused attention from organized leftist women and men. Their central call was a regional unity to fight imperialism, but without feminist demands for women's political, legal, and economic rights, imperialism could easily return or, to use the term in the resolution, *adapt* to the new conditions of local or national self-rule.

The second conference appeal targeted women of the imperialist countries, naming the United States, Britain, France, and Holland in particular. They described the shared violence and losses of colonial wars that affected all women. But they added a special ethical imperative: "Do not allow yourselves to be accomplices of our murderers! ... Do not permit our sons to kill each other! Stop colonial wars! Insist that your governments recall the troops from Vietnam, Indonesia, Malaya, Korea."[9] Motherhood in this appeal could not be conceived outside of war: women must refuse to raise sons who become murderers. The appeal linked home to the theater of war. Both appeals relied on a shared analysis of imperialism—and which countries were imperialist—for two powerful aims. First, they celebrated the leadership of Asian women fighting British, American, French, and Dutch colonial militarism. Second, they promoted an internationalism led by these revolutionary anti-colonial women.

But there was another internationalist feminist strategy that emerged from the conference, one that was not represented in either of the 1949 AWC appeals. It sought to build a multi-class international women's movement for peace using the language of radical motherhood. This third strategy was a more public path that was integral to WIDF's active debates before, during, and after the 1949 conference in Beijing, which had proponents from around the world, including the Union of Soviet Socialist Republics, the United States, and Sweden. A large delegation of women from the US Congress of American Women (CAW) attended WIDF's Budapest Congress and listened to Cai's speech in 1948. Three of them—two African American, one white—also joined the Asian Women's Conference a year later: Ada Jackson, Eslanda Robeson, and Betty Millard. Millard's diary notes revealed her own feelings about how activists had to take into account their own location within imperialism. "Yesterday she (Parfinova) said she thought I looked unhappy at references to A.I. [American imperialism]—and wanted to know, did I—which was her way, I later realized of saying she's talked to Olga [Milosevic in the WIDF secretariat] and wanted to know what about it."[10] This reference to Millard's discomfort was linked to the conference resolutions for the Asian Women's Conference. It echoes the discomfort that surfaced the month before during the November, 1949 meeting of the WIDF Council members held in Moscow. That meeting's resolutions distinguished between fighting a country's imperialist government and fighting the people of the country, who may or may not support their nation's imperialism.

In 1948, at the Second Congress in Budapest, CAW participants as well as Sweden's representative Andrea Andreen, also an important leader within WIDF, raised the difficulty of organizing around WIDF resolutions that named the United States as the central imperialist aggressor and sought more diplomacy. "But we may perhaps change our propaganda a little, not condemn the West so categorically.... If there were an equal percentage of members in the Western countries now to that of the Eastern countries, our resolutions would be formulated with more prudence than they are made now."[11] Members from the United States said that the intensified political context of the Cold War would make their organization's survival impossible. However, WIDF's final resolution in 1948 *did* name the United States as the primary agent of postwar imperialism: "American monopolists seek to dominate the world. With the aid of the Marshall Plan, they deprive nations of their sovereignty, turning people into servants of the American warmakers."[12] The directness of this resolution, and the resolve of CAW to bring it to American women, had the consequences they foresaw. By 1949, CAW members were charged with subversion by the House Un-American Activities Committee (HUAC) and all members had to register as foreign agents. By 1950, CAW was banned and dismantled. Yet in 1951, these same women created new political groups for peace, and put their bodies on the line to stop the US-led war and occupation of Korea.[13]

In the context of heightened anti-communism, motherhood functioned as a mode of address to women that sought to be an acceptable public register for anti-imperialist organizing of the greatest numbers of women. After the conference, WIDF gave clear directions for ways to draw more women in Europe and the United States into the movement to end colonialism through invocations to mothers who sought peace. "The anxiety of the mothers is increasing and is expressing itself in their fears and their protests. To transform the mothers' anxiety into coordinated and concrete action; to show them their immense responsibility for the defense of their little ones' lives; to convince them that they can and must be themselves the best architects of their children's happiness; all this comprises one of the most important tasks which we democratic women must set ourselves."[14] The campaigns around the world on March 8, International Women's Day, sought to heighten women's commitment to survival, against imperialist war, through the invocation of motherhood and peace.

Archival records about the Asian Women's Conference are scattered; they are found in WIDF's publication, *Information Bulletins,* in the typed daily reports sent to WIDF member women's groups, in the newspaper articles published in sympathetic presses from Morocco to Cuba, and in the notebooks of delegates and conference guests. Detailed reports by the spies of the United States and Britain sought to name names and track its activism. There was no official record, such as those published by WIDF after the Second Congress in Budapest, a book that pulled together all the speeches, rejoinders, appeals, resolutions, and interventions with delegates' names and organizations. Instead, there was one special issue of the *Information Bulletin* dedicated to the conference speeches and resolutions. The bulk of these conference traces consist of the country reports by delegates that describe the particular conditions of their struggles.

These country reports are vital building blocks to reconstruct the profound theoretical intervention made during the Asian Women's Conference. Rather than simply describing the specific struggles' strategies or tactics, country reports at the Asian Women's Conference solidified the conjunctural analysis for women's anti-imperialist internationalism. They stated that the fight against colonialism must be at its center, and the women on the frontlines of that struggle must lead the way forward for the internationalist women's movement. All women of the world were encouraged to take an active part in the fight. The *Information Bulletins* and the daily typed reports provide another window into the conference since they detailed the conference resolutions and appeals to the wider circle of WIDF's solidarity. They reveal the outcome of the conference: its theory for women's internationalist praxis.

ANTI-IMPERIALIST APPEALS IN PRACTICE

The conference configured examples of how to coordinate internationalist women's activism across geopolitical borders in its speakers' reports. For example, in the case of Indonesian anti-imperialist internationalism, Lillah Suripno was the Indonesian delegate to the Asian Women's Conference and a member of the Indonesian Communist Party (PKI). Suripno spoke immediately before Maria Lips-Odinot, known as Rie, who was the chairwoman of the Dutch Women's Movement and a communist. Together, their reports illustrated what concerted anti-imperialist solidarity should be. Suripno emphasized Indonesian women's full participation in the fight against the Dutch military attack.[15] Indonesian women were part of all anti-imperialist resistance movements in the region, as fighters as well as in logistical support, surveillance, communication, and infrastructure. She emphasized the role of women in these battles: "Indonesian women fight with arms in hand for national independence!"[16] She also reminded her audience of two points: first was that Indonesia sought full independence from all foreign intervention. Second, she emphasized the importance of the Dutch movement's refusal to support their government's occupation of Indonesia. For her part, Lips-Odinot described Dutch women's opposition at the shipyards sending off arms to colonial soldiers in Indonesia. The women's movement in the Netherlands must take its directions and fervor from Indonesian women's demands, she said. For any hope of freedom, theirs had to be a unified struggle with common aims.

All of the women who took the trans-Siberian train to Beijing attended a WIDF board meeting held in Moscow in October 1949, six weeks before the Asian Women's Conference. In Moscow, the seeds of WIDF's two-fold praxis was given a pragmatic flexibility, characterized by delegate Marion Ramelson of England: "To work to draw all active women into active struggle, and to achieve this, it is recommended to take into account the national peculiarities of the movement in each country."[17] The women's movements across the world could develop solidarity actions to coordinate their anti-colonial activism in many possible forms. However, women in imperialist countries had to oppose imperialism from within their ideologies, economies, and governmental policies. Solidified between 1945 and 1949, this two-fold internationalist praxis challenged and ultimately presaged the full support for national independence movements by the previously pro-colonial wings of European communist parties, including the Dutch and French ones.

At the AWC, Jeannette Vermeersch, a leader in WIDF and the Union of French Women as well as a member of parliament,

Figure 4. Ho Thi Minh and Jeannette Vermeersch embrace during the Asian Women's Conference, Beijing, December 1949. Photo courtesy of Sophia Smith Archives, Smith College.

emphasized the intertwined class struggle of anti-colonialism in France.

> It is undeniable that the armed struggle of the Viet Nam people is helping the working class and the democratic movement in France to a very large extent... Imperialism will be defeated in every case if we want it to be. Peace works for the people. And if, in spite of our efforts, the imperialists want to launch a new war in Europe against the USSR, and want to use our countries as war bases, then we are sure that the people of France and Italy will not fight in the imperialists' war, but will turn against the imperialists and put an end to their shameful aggression.[18]

Ho Thi Minh, the sole Vietnamese delegate able to reach Beijing in time for the conference, embraced her after her speech.

Within a month after the Asian Women's Conference ended, Vermeersch gave a scathing speech in the French parliament against colonialism. On January 25, 1950, the Union of French Women launched a national day of organizing for the Day of Struggle Against the War in Viet Nam that included asking steel, dock, and railways workers to resist the production and the distribution of armaments in the war economy. Two days later, Vermeersch shredded the language of humanitarianism surrounding the French colonial war in Vietnam. In a speech republished and distributed around the world, she addressed the French National Assembly, a body that included Communist Party members. "The Vietnamese people are fighting a just war," she said, "a war in the defense against your aggression, a war of national liberation. You are fighting an unjust war, a colonial war, a war of aggression."[19]

The conference resolutions were carefully negotiated ones that navigated the rapidly changing context of Asian anti-imperialism. Communist Party of China leaders, such as Liu Shaoqi, argued against a resolution in the Asian Women's Conference that emphasized open fights for women's legal rights in Asia. According to Dieter Herzig, Liu argued that Asian women who openly sought the legal rights to marriage reform, equal pay, or land rights would immediately be targeted by colonial regimes, and thus a direct demand for women's rights was too dangerous.[20] Campaigns for legal reforms in these repressive colonial contexts would lead to women activists' imprisonment or death rather than build women's multi-class unity in the region. Women's participation in Asian liberation movements was necessarily underground. Instead of legal reforms, Liu Shaoqi favored a resolution for regional unity and support for armed combat. Even these general demands, he argued, had to be kept secret in order to ensure the safety of women in active struggles across Asia and Africa.

Liu's hesitance about Asian women's open advocacy for equal rights in the colonial context was strategic, not out of principle. But it was still a difficult issue to navigate as delegates from the Asian Women's Conference sought to nimbly guide women's struggles through their appeals and resolutions. In the 1940s, many of WIDF's international demands for women's rights, such as for the right to own property and divorce at will, assumed that women already enjoyed some form (even if limited) of representative governance. These aspirations were shared by Asian, Latin American, and African women. However, for those under colonial occupation, women's rights were woven into the aspiration for a socialist government that affirmed their rights to exist, to exercise leadership, to have a voice, and to self-determination. Anti-colonial women's movements across the world fought for both rights and deeply representative self-determination simultaneously. As the shared platform for the internationalist women's movement, WIDF, they argued, had to accurately mirror their commitments.

The AWC conference resolutions reflected the communists' two-camp analysis of postwar alignments, as mentioned, but these strategies for an internationalist anti-imperialist women's movement were fueled by more complex forces of power than simply negotiations among national communist parties. They also exceed the frame of the international women's organization of WIDF. World unity among women opposing imperialism developed from Asian and African women's struggle over a longer period of time than the four years after the war in Europe ended in 1945. The moment to demand the reins of self-governance emerged with the end of the European war for countries like India, Pakistan, Vietnam, and Malaysia, but the organizational strength behind this demand lay in rural organizing that began much earlier.

In the years after the Asian Women's Conference, women increasingly became the public face of revolutionary, anticolonial peace through a rhetoric of radical motherhood. Even when couched in the language of family, this praxis maintained that anticolonial struggles were won and lost by the barrel of the gun. However, this bridge between two different visions for feminist internationalism was fraught. One, represented by the 1949 AWC conference resolutions, centered the knowledge of peasant women's struggle against colonialism and the landed systems of rule that preceded it. The other was a rhetorical strategy that sought to build global linkages through radical motherhood. Suzy Kim argues that anti-war discourses of motherhood in the WIDF "tried to bridge the Cold War divide through maternal strategies."[21] As a strategy, it sought to circumvent rising anticommunism across the West and build meaningful connections with women in colonial struggles in Asia, Latin America, and Africa through shared social roles as mothers. Their demands for a just peace alongside a vision for revolutionary motherhood emerged from women's country reports during the AWC.

In 1949, the delegates to the AWC deepened this two-part vision for feminist, socialist internationalism. A third part of this strategy was the role of women in socialist countries, most notably China and the Soviet Union, who provided material support, guidance, and inspiration for the horizon of the internationalist women's movement. These were the democratic ideals that fostered women's equal rights and equal access to all the fruits and work of the public sphere. Many of the speakers at the conference ended their speeches with invocations to the life possibilities of Asian Soviets like Uzbekistan. They emphasized the stark improvements socialism made for the education of children, the abolishment of child labor, and the literacy rates of everyone, including women. Nadezhda Parfenova, who joined the Young Communist League as an orphaned child, led the Soviet Union's fraternal delegation. In her speech, she celebrated the inspiration of Chinese leadership:

> This conference has a historic significance. It is the first time in the history of the women's movement that the representatives of progressive organizations of fourteen Asian countries have met in conference to exchange their experiences and discuss effective means of intensifying the women's struggle for national independence and for the improvement of their children's living conditions. This has become possible as a result of the development of the national liberation in the colonial and dependent countries, and primarily thanks to the victory of the democratic forces in China. The victory of the Chinese people is the source of inspiration for millions of enslaved men and women in the colonial and dependent countries in their struggle for liberation from the imperialist yoke.[22]

The official appeal from the conference extended that inspiration more widely across Asia: "The women of China and Mongolia, of North Korea and the liberated areas of Viet Nam have obtained equal political and economic rights. The women are playing an important role in the life of these countries. They are looking toward the future with calm confidence. From these examples, we the women of Asia, are convinced that only when people are masters of their destiny can real emancipation for women be realized."[23]

The geopolitics of capitalism bifurcated its strategy into two main parts: women's activism outside imperial centers, and women's activism inside those centers—as accomplices in struggle, activism in these political locations were coordinated, but not identical. However, the struggles and demands shaped by colonized women led in both locations of activism. In rural and urban colonial territories, the erasure of older forms of women's rights and community power were a necessary kindling for colonialism. The suppression of women's rights fueled, and then congealed, colonial control over occupied territories. Women's rights had to be at the heart of the anti-colonial project of systemically loosening the grip of imperialism on the world, if that project was to succeed. At its best, internationalist feminism as women's regional anticolonial solidarity across the Third World could dig the grave for colonialism. Western women's staunch rejection of their own nations' imperialism could help bury it for good.

REVOLUTIONARY MOTHERHOOD AND POLITICAL REPRODUCTION

Marxist theories of reproductive labor, including reproduction of the species, of peace as a just peace, and of motherhood as an activist subjectivity provide the scaffolding for women's internationalism. WIDF publications, especially noticeably after 1949, repeatedly used the language of motherhood—a social role accorded to women—to describe the political subjectivity of women. In correlation to their focus on mothers and motherhood, they fought for the rights of children and a fuller, more just childhood. Their reporting about childhood under colonialism was particularly stark. The Iranian delegate, Mahine Faroqi, spoke about children's lifetime of labor, from the age of five onwards, and their imprisonment and torture if they resisted. Taruna Bose from India emphasized the lack of the most basic education for children under colonialism. The lie of civilization under colonial rule shaped children's lives from birth. The needs of children for schools, daycares, nutrition, and health care directly opposed the war economy in state expenditure and state priorities. To fight for children's basic needs could dismantle the huge state expenditures for military dominance. If "peace" invoked the end of imperialist aggression in WIDF's terms, "motherhood" included the Marxist analysis of reproductive labor. A leftist women's organization like WIDF used motherhood as a location for the politicization of women.

In the Marxist tradition of analysis, the capitalist character of productive labor (that is, paid work) must be understood alongside reproductive labor (that is, the unpaid work of generational and daily survival). Under capitalism, the unwaged character of what capitalism deemed women's biological destiny—reproductive labor, or "women's work"—shifts additional profits from workers' paid work to the capitalists. The more that capitalist ideologies erase the value and even the *work* of daily reproduction, by calling it love, or by calling it nothing at all, the more invisible that labor becomes, even to the workers themselves. The social value of women plummets; as reproductive laborers their labor has no exchange value. Even when they enter the paid workforce, women's depressed social value is used to pay them less than men for their work. Yet, in capitalism workers alone must reproduce themselves. As Marx famously described the freedom of workers in capitalism, they are free to starve.

Under capitalism, women's unwaged and unrecognized reproductive labor erodes their value as waged workers. Capitalism uses women to lower wages and working conditions for all workers. Working-class women become the enemy of working-class men. In the faulty logic of this divide-and-conquer tactic, women, and not the owners of the means of production, leach men's wages as unproductive wives and daughters. Women, not factory owners, lower men's wages as workers on the margins, since women are forced to take any job at any wage. Unity among the working classes requires ideologies of solidarity to confront capitalist logics of division. Unity cannot stop at national borders or union membership, but must remain strong among all workers, across all geographic boundaries. But that unity faces powerfully enforced barriers of difference: of race, of gender, and of geography.

Under capitalism, enshrining motherhood as women's ideal domestic destiny promises some social value to middle-class married women. However, motherhood as a domestic ideal for women also ensures that women who must also take waged work to survive remain on the lowest rung of the hierarchy—tarnished both as bad mothers/inferior women and threatening waged workers. The labor regimes of colonialism and systemic racism compound these gendered orders of value. As WIDF members testified during this period, working-class black women in places like the United States and working women in colonies and former colonies took the least secure, most exploited jobs—jobs in some contexts that were barely waged at all.

In the pro-socialist context of the Women's International Democratic Federation in the 1940s and 1950s, motherhood, like peace, was complex. Motherhood, in part, invoked a possibility long denied to oppressed and exploited women. During the anti-colonial insurgencies that exploded in colonies and former colonies around the world during this period, motherhood as a site of value and pleasure was an aspiration. Motherhood, in WIDF publications from 1945 onwards, also sought to invoke a universal value for women's unpaid labor of reproduction, rather than as women's weakness in the market or a marker of women's lower social worth. As a universal value, rather than a privilege of class or race, motherhood in this sense required a different order of being than it ever had in capitalism. In the context of WIDF, motherhood also emphasized women's economic and a political power, and the creation of a world, a pro-socialist world, that recognized and supported the socially necessary labor of mothers.

What WIDF's use of "motherhood" as a pro-socialist invocation leaves out, however, is the centrality of motherhood and other familial ties to the strength of anti-colonial movements in Asia and around the world. It leaves out political reproductive labor by activist women. The delegates at the conference represented their larger communist, left-wing or anti-colonial movements of women and men. Activist memoirs and interviews of women from these movements, saturate their stories with the importance of family networks and close family friends that made their politics possible. Agnes Khoo collected interviews with communist and pro-communist anti-colonial women activists in Malaya. Again and again, they told stories of how they entered the revolutionary movement and sustained their activism against the harsh repression of their Japanese and the British occupiers through familial relationships. For example, Chen Xiu Zhu, a Chinese worker in Malaysia, described her organizing methods in the Communist Party of Malaya (CPM). "I reminded myself that I must try my best to fulfil whatever tasks the Party gave me. We organized mothers whose sons had joined the guerillas (the fighting contingents living in the mountains) and the wives of husbands who had also joined."[24] These stories often mentioned the children these women were forced to leave behind in the care of others. Mothers, like wives, sisters, and daughters, brought relational ties of support, inspiration, and political consciousness to the growing anti-colonial movements. These were also ties of loss. I have read no memoirs or interviews where family relationships forced women to join anti-colonial or communist politics. Instead, these connections, even if of tacit support by young women's mothers, are a kind of reproductive political glue of these dangerous political decisions to join the movement. Motherhood, particularly women's mothers (rather than their own acts of mothering), provided material, daily, and substantive support to the reproduction of revolutionary movements themselves.

A JUST PEACE

In 1948, delegates to the WIDF's Second Congress gave their full support for Cai Chang's unapologetic embrace of armed freedom movements as the necessary response to colonial intransigence and exploitation. Thus, in 1949, the debate among the delegates at the Asian Women's Conference was not about the violence itself, but about supportive actions and strategies for a meaningful internationalism. At this gathering, Asian and African delegates solidified a praxis that amplified internationalist women's *material* solidarity for these armed struggles. Cai's analysis of postwar imperialism and the struggles against it ended with three tasks for women: peace, self-determination, and what she called a true democracy that eradicated poverty and starvation to provide "the freedom to live under human conditions."[25]

The Soviet Union exemplified the goals of true democracy, and inspired people's movements around the world. Cai wholeheartedly lauded its material and ideological support for anti-colonialism and anti-imperialism. By 1949, Cai's analysis continued to carry weight within the WIDF. Deng Yingchao delivered

Figure 5. Cai Chang and Marie-Claude Vaillant-Couturier, Asian Women's Conference, Beijing, December 1949. Photo courtesy of Sophia Smith Archives, Smith College.

an address on the second day of the conference that elaborated on Cai's assessment from the previous year. "China's experiences tell us that it is only through the resolute struggle of the armed people against armed counter-revolution that the oppressed people in the colonies and semi-colonies may attain their freedom."[26] Like Cai Chang, Deng held a powerful leadership role in the women's movement of China. She was the vice-chairwoman and co-founder of the All-China Democratic Women's Federation (which became the All-China Women's Federation) in March, 1949. Like many communist women of her generation, she joined the May Fourth feminist movement in the 1920s, activism that led her to join the CCP in 1925. Also, she was married to Zhou Enlai, the Premier of the People's

Republic of China. Deng was a leading member of the group that drafted the 1950 Marriage Law, the first law enacted in communist China.[27] As scholar Wang Zheng details, Deng provided careful leadership skills to strengthen the impact of the ACWF's demands for women's equality in the policies and laws of the new communist state.[28]

Deng's endorsement of the necessity of armed struggle echoed other recent internationalist gatherings in Asia, most notably the World Federation of Democratic Youth and Students (WFDY) held in Kolkata in February, 1948. At this meeting for Asian youth and students, the debate about violent resistance to colonialism that emerged surprised even its organizers.[29] The WFDY conference resolutions demanded no compromise with imperialists in the region, an outcome the conference organizers had not predicted in advance. Within months, military resistance to colonialism broke out in Myanmar (March 1948), Malaysia (June 1948), and Indonesia (September 1948). By 1949, vast sections of Vietnam gained a formal independence that proved fragile in the face of French determination to hold onto the territory as its colony.

The broken promises for a slow transition to full independence proffered after the end of World War II by England in Burma and Malaysia, by France in Vietnam, and by Holland in Indonesia resulted in armed resistance. In 1948 and 1949, the Indonesian independence movement had taken up the few arms available to them, through channels that led from India through Burma and from China through Vietnam. Many rural people fought only with handmade wooden weapons and explosives left over from the end of Japanese occupation. Meanwhile, the French, British, and Dutch actively colluded to support each other's military counterinsurgency assaults by lending arms, military ships and planes, and other equipment they had used against the Japanese during the war.

Colonial wars in Asia had direct consequences for American financial capitalism as well. Here Deng echoed other conference delegates in her assessment that American imperialists seek "to convert all the Asiatic Countries into their colonies and use them as aggressive bases in a third world war."[30] This second element of American colonialism was not identical to older colonial powers: colonialism was still about the extraction of wealth and about the exploitation of workers, but it was also about creating compliant territories to stage planetary war. Under financial capitalism, with its graft of ever-greater profits from natural resources and people's labor, imperial countries no longer sought land for direct rule, but as military launchpads. The shift towards what WIDF publications designated "puppet governments" marked the retreat from the subject status of colonial countries under colonizing countries. National independence, as delegates from India, Indonesia, and Myanmar knew well, was hamstrung by the dominance of Euro-American financial capital and by the looming military presence of imperialist powers.

With devastating prescience of the global war to come, Pak Chŏng-ae described South Korea as a site of occupation with its American-backed strongman, Syngman Rhee. She explained the imperial significance of Korea for US domination of the Asian region beyond Japan and the reasons why the United States would go to any lengths to block its reunification. As Pak Chŏng-ae emphasized, the importance of North and South Korea intensified after the Communist Party of China defeated the Guomindang in China's civil war. Her report described the US occupation by proxy:

Our partisan units [in South Korea], fully supported by the people, won brilliant victories in battle. That is not all. The inner organization of Syngman Rhee's puppet army has begun to disintegrate. Opposing the traitorous policy of SYNGMANN RHEE [sic], soldiers have courageously revolted, and joined the people, fighting with the guerillas.[31]

North Korea and South Korea became separate states in 1948. Border skirmishes began with the formation of a border along the 38th parallel north. Women and men joined the self-defense units in North Korea that fought off cross-border incursions, as well as looting and arson of food supplies.[32] Suzy Kim described the frustration of people living along the border. "One peasant woman in her late forties complained that the guard units had no countermeasure despite the kidnapping, claiming she would join them 'if they would be willing to go kill 'em.'"[33] WIDF's multiple international conferences, the meetings that delegates held with local clubs after they returned home, and the publication of WIDF's conference reports allowed internationalist women to frame their knowledge of the world from the perspective of leftist women's struggles. Korea as a theater of war was not a conflict of Soviet or Chinese aggression, nor of North Korean intractability, as US and European media portrayed it. Chŏng-ae's analysis provided a very different understanding from the Euro-American consensus.

In December 1949, five months before the US invasion of Korea, Pak Chŏng-ae described a state of ongoing military battle against US occupation of South Korea. In her report, the war began with the imperialist occupation (by the United States) of Korea by a proxy government (led by Syngman Rhee) at the very moment that the Japanese occupation of Korea ended. Syngman

Rhee's government undermined democratic rule, crushed any dissent to his rule, and outlawed communism. The occupying forces negotiated what they said would be a temporary border between the two regions of Korea, the 38th parallel. That border was to be a placeholder until a national election. For a variety of reasons that election was never held, in large part due to the deep unpopularity of Syngman Rhee's government even in the region south of the 38th parallel. In Pak Chŏng-ae's report, North Koreans, and many pro-socialist South Koreans, fought an anti-imperialist war that sought to end the neocolonial occupation of the entire region by the United States.

WOMEN'S ANTI-COLONIAL ACTIVISM AND GLOBAL MILITARISM IN AFRICA

The conjunctural analysis of women's activism in 1949 drew on women's country reports and the experience of anti-colonial struggles among women. For example, two fraternal delegates from Africa centered the lessons from organizing in rural and urban locations to support the importance of organizing among the masses of women, rather than only among the most educated women or those already most connected to anti-colonial movements. Techniques of organizing rural women emerged across the globe: in China, India, Vietnam and elsewhere, these methods were shared to better draw the largest masses of women into the center of anti-imperialist organizing through local struggles.

Baya Bouhoune Allaouchiche, general secretary of the Algerian Women's Union, presented a clear picture of postwar imperialism and the solidarity Algerian women practiced. "Algeria is in fact a colony of France with political, economic and social inequalities and the crushing of national culture," she said, directly contradicting any evasions of Algeria's special status under French colonial rule. "War (is) being prepared before (the) eyes of people. Algerian troops have been sent to Vietnam and Algerian women have protested against this."[34]Allaouchiche details the politics of imperialism, the place of Algerian women and men, and an Algerian women's solidarity of complicity. Algerian peasant women and men drove away the recruiting agents who offered cash for their sons' enlistment into the colonial military. This solidarity laid bare the colonial relations of war. Algerian soldiers were trained by the French to crush the Vietnamese independence struggle. Algerian women's solidarity assumed accountability for the mercenary actions of Algerian soldiers and thus protested the use of Algerians by the French against the Vietnamese.

In the words of Gisele Rabesahala, the delegate from Madagascar, "drenched in blood, the people refuse to be accomplices of the imperialists."[35] In this women's movement, colonialism was shorn of its veneer of local self-governance, its promises of women's education, or its erasure of state-planned starvation and the dispossession of peasants' land. Colonialism was war. These refusals to edicts of colonialism, led by rural and urban women, were not simply solidarity actions of nationalism. The actions themselves demanded confrontations with gender norms of public behavior, and more broadly, the public stage for political action itself. The very possibility of refusing to allow their sons to enlist forced a confrontation with women's access to public space, public voice, and autonomy as anti-colonialism.

Feminism, in the leftist diction of the time, referred to women's legal and political rights shorn of any attention to (if not outright refusal to demand) the economic transformation of capitalism. The revolutionary refusals of colonialism described by delegates like Allaouchiche, however, reframed feminism and demands for women's legal and political rights as demands made meaningful *through* anti-colonialism as a movement for people's self-determination and radically different world orders. She also told a story about the revolutionary persistence among rural Algerian women. Because industrial crops for international markets supplanted food grain for the local population, she said, "people of *Kabyl* origin, to whom I belong, have been pushed back to the mountains where olive and fig trees grow but where the soil is stony, fertile plots are rare, and communications difficult."[36] The story of widespread unemployment, landlessness and hunger went hand in hand with women's growing revolutionary consciousness. Allaouchiche described one woman who survived a miners' strike in which her husband participated by selling everything they had to feed their children, but she had a dilemma came when her pregnancy came to term. "When her time came for delivery, she did not even have an alfa grass mat on which to deliver her child. She went to her mother who said, 'Go to your home. You must give birth at your place. You must show yourself to be courageous so that your husband remains calm in the struggle he leads. This struggle, and all others, will allow your child to live free and happy.'"[37] Algerian rural women's support for the revolution had an important religious character, especially for Algerian communist women who were often of European descent and from either Jewish or Christian backgrounds. Allaouchiche, herself from an Algerian Muslim family, closed her story with its lesson: "Muslim women, especially, are entering the struggle."[38] As women at the 1949 conference fully appreciated, without poor, illiterate, and often rural women, the revolutionary movement in Algeria would remain small and embattled.

Gisele Rabesahala described the conditions in Madagascar, giving details of enormous profit for French, British and American firms, and of devastation for the people of Madagascar. "In 1944," she illustrated with stark simplicity, "there were 25,000 more deaths than births."[39] Colonial devastation also explained the growing militance of women from African countries. The refusal to accept colonialism after war led to a more united political organization of the people. Colonial forces cracked down with brutal force, from their own desperation in a battle already lost. She told the story of Rasoanoro Zele, a woman who in the face of French disapproval fought for election in the Provincial Assembly of Tananarive. She lost, but her election proved "in spite of the repression which is still raging, the confidence of the people of Madagascar went to her, the representative of their struggle for national independence."[40]

Delegates to the AWC acted as theorists, propagandists, communicators, and reporters. They sought to transform their peoples' hard-won knowledge into strength of action. They sought to communicate the knife's edge of colonialism and imperialism to unite women across the world. Their particularities shaped their tactics and strategies to win their battles each day, each week, each year. In China, most of the women did not fight on the battlefields. They joined the struggle by increasing production of food, equipment, and other basic human needs. In Vietnam, women played a myriad of roles, including engaging in active combat against the French forces, but took the lead in international propaganda work to convince the world to stand down and drop their arms. In Indonesia, women focused on rural areas, to politicize rural women through literacy and other campaigns for basic rights. In India, women demanded that their independent state address the poorest peoples' needs rather than ignore them once independence had been won. As building blocks to fight imperialism, they shared their knowledge with their sisters in struggle.

CHAPTER FOUR

To Save the World

Gita Bandyopadhyay was an exceptional activist: an early fighter for communism when the movement was still in its first decades.[1] Her activism began when she was thirteen years old. She was born to a landed family in Shibnibash, Bengal. Her paternal grandmother, Katyayani Devi, fought for the rights of young widows and deserted housewives in the locality, to the dismay of the other Brahmin families in the locality.[2] As Gita described her, "she had such authority in the village that she could make a tiger and a deer drink from the same pond."[3] Gita was brave like her grandmother, and when she joined the communist movement in the late 1930s, she gave up an entire lifetime of comfort and ease. Her first protest sought the release of political prisoners from the jail in the Andamans. Though arrested by the British authorities, to her searing disappointment she was released because at thirteen years old she was considered underage.

Gita Bandyopadhyay joined the Communist Party of India through its cover: the Workers Party. When in college, she joined the Chhatri Sangh, the leftist women's student organization linked to the larger All India Federation of Students. In addition, Gita was an early member of the famed leftist women's organization the Mahila Atmaraksha Samiti (MARS), translated as the Women's Self-Respect, or more commonly Women's Self-Defense, League.[4] While still in her twenties, she joined the central offices of the Women's International Democratic Federation in Paris, France to help build an anti-imperialist women's movement. This is her story, but it is also one of women's leftist solidarity that was built on their commonalties and their differences in the landscape of the end of one war, World War Two, and the continuance of imperial wars that sought to hold on to their colonial territories against the will of the people who lived in those countries.

Bandyopadhyay was from the enfranchised middle class in Bengal, India. Her family valued education for girls and boys. She lived abroad with her family and went to school in Malaysia, until her mother died suddenly and her father sent her to live with extended family in Kolkata. She joined Kamala Girls School without knowing the Bengali alphabet, but she and her siblings "managed to mug up the alphabets quite fast."[5] She went to college, studied, and learned. But she took a conscious chance and was not *of* the middle class. By the time she had finished college, she had married someone of her own choice, and divorced. Middle-class goals were not hers, not necessarily. For parts of her life, she lived and organized among the mill workers and the very poor in the Bengal Delta, a marshy region that had minimal desalinated land for farming, and endless mosquitoes as vectors for malaria and other mundane, deadly diseases. The district was also a hotbed of radicalism since the turn of the century. Later she returned to Kolkata as a communist women's organizer, an artist, and an educator.

Gita Bandyopadhyay studied the same scholarly texts as others—novels, mathematics, science and geography in school. Marx, too, probably the *Communist Manifesto* since the Bengali translation was passed hand to hand throughout the region at this time. Study circles shared this and other Marxist books, always by candlelight, at night, in secret, alongside one's comrades.[6] Her communist analysis of colonialism meant she must understand its origins and purpose for capitalism, not simply as a geo-political or historical aggression. She had to understand the larger schemes that crafted the local manifestations in Kolkata, in Bengal, and in India. There was a world outside this colony that Gita also must understand in relation to her own conditions. Other colonizers, other colonized. The end of colonialism for communists demanded a scooping together of all those struggles, all those particularities chipped away and cast aside by capitalism. Gita studied but also became one of these fragments once she cast her solidarity with the working classes, organizing with the labor unions formed in the jute mills and coal factories that studded the Houghly River.

Gita joined the struggle at an exceptional time. Another imperialist war emanated from Europe's continent fueled by land acquisition and genocide. As with the global war earlier in the twentieth century, this one fought for turf in Europe and around the world, but mostly for the raw capital that solidified imperial pre-eminence within global capitalism. The bereft in the colonies during this battle of hubris were not the middle class, nor the gentry. Farmers, artisans, fisherfolk, craftspeople, weavers, brickmakers, miners, jute workers, market women, food sellers, folk singers, goat herders, painters, potters, iron smelters, forest dwellers suffered most from the wrath of world wars. Their livelihoods were swept away by the ravenous needs of war in Europe. All foodstuffs from the colonies moved North by dictat, not by chance or the invisible hand of supply and demand. All boats, even small wooden crafts for the Bengal Delta byways, were commandeered by the overlords.

When starvation struck in Bengal, it seemed sudden to some, chalked up to a regionally bad harvest, a hoarding of grain reserves. But famine struck colonized swaths of the world at the same time: Senegal, Algeria, Tunisia, Iran, and Morocco all faced unprecedented food shortages during the war. In Bengal, an onslaught of destitute people flooded into the cities in 1943 and 1944. People like Gita, who sought to listen to the lives, wants, needs, and desires of the workers, knew its onset was jumpstarted by war, and the military bases mushrooming along the borders of Burma and across the colonized territories of world. War exacerbated endemic want that defined ordinary people's place in the hierarchy of needs. Starvation for Bengal's rural masses began before the poor rice harvest late in 1942. That harvest was the trigger, not the cause. The tinder, not the gun.

Gita joined the struggle at an ordinary time. "All around us was the silent, careful footsteps of Socialism," she described. She and her classmates were "influenced by her [the Bengali teacher Sudha Ray] and let ourselves go in the tide of Socialism at the mere age of thirteen. One moment there would be a call to defy Section 144—in the next we'd be in a class on Karl Marx's *Communist Manifesto*, learning to look at an international revolution together—all in all, it was an enchanting atmosphere."[7] The anti-imperialist movement enjoyed long shadows into the nineteenth century. Women had participated in sabotage, assassination and revolution for many decades, not only in Bengal, but there too. There were many clandestine armed groups, such as Yugantar and Anushilan Samiti, which were active in Bengal in the first quarter of the twentieth century. Their members mainly came from the ranks of urban, educated, and unemployed youth—including unmarried young women—and they mostly carried out isolated killings of colonial British officers.

In the 1940s, Gita joined the workers' movement to listen to the workers' wants and to make manifest their needs and desires. From this commitment to the working class and peasantry, she sought to end colonialism as the engine of capitalism. In the Marxist analysis of Gita and her comrades, colonialism was a tool for capitalism, one answer to the system's contradictions of supply and demand, overproduction and underconsumption. Colonialism was an integral part of capitalism, and not simply a coercive system of unequal governance by a white supremacist foreign hand. Instead, colonialism fed the ravenous maw of capitalism by creating new markets, new workers, and thus additional surplus value, additional profit wrung from labor exacted to make its wheels go round.

Colonialism referred to the outside control of colony trade: the raw materials shorn from the continent, of timber, of cotton, of tea shipped wholesale to Britain. Anticolonial movements of all stripes in the 1940s agreed that this practice must end. In addition, the captive markets of India and other colonized lands must cease. Indians could produce their own cloth and make their own salt free of British taxation. Nationalist movements agreed: until British occupation, the people of the subcontinent had done so. The anti-colonial movements in which Gita swam demanded a more risky politics of refusal. These movements sought to throw a spanner in the engines of capitalism itself. Organizing the industrial workers of jute mills and coal mines alongside the landless agricultural workers and small landholding peasants was critical to this vision.

To listen to the workers, as communist and labor movements sought to do, complicated the knowledge of ledgers and accounts, taxes and accruals in the hands of educated middle class Indians. To listen to the workers during the 1940s was not an act alone, it had to be learned—first, by spending time and energy alongside working class people. It meant turning one's middle-class gifts to other ends than a smooth transition from colonial governance to a nationalist one. The system itself needed new logics, new beneficiaries, and most of all new horizons.

Industrial capitalism of the nineteenth century demanded everything the world had to give. Ships and railroads required unending old-growth forests. Factories required fuel dug from every wellspring of the earth. Weapons of greater range and destruction needed ever more complex natural resources, combined in chemically innovative ways. Gold was still valuable. Jewels still glittered. Land still measured the worth of a sovereign. But in industrial capitalism, mobility of things was the key to ever-expanding riches. The colonialism that Gita sought to end was in transition in the 1940s. The tools that served industrial capitalism were transmogrifying to better feed finance capitalism.

The colonialism of industrial capitalism anchored the monopoly over the raw materials, production, and markets of things sold for profit. Gita and her comrades developed theories about colonialism under finance capitalism that sought to monopolize the production and circulation of financial instruments themselves.[8] Capital as investment in a country or region became even more scarce in newly independent nations after the formal end to colonial domination. The need to understand this new order within capitalism fell heaviest on the shoulders of Gita and her comrades for a simple reason. Their movements of people faced the blunt end of capitalism's spasms first.

The source of value in industrial capitalism was the labor of workers wrenched from their bodies. Finance capitalism, as with industrial capitalism, still relied on the expropriation of labor value away from the workers and farmers who did the work. But finance capitalism was more efficient at peeling away the layers of profit from the middle-dealers, and at congealing those profits to the very few at the top. The monopoly over land and industry as the means of production congealed with the monopoly over the circulation of capital itself as a commodity that was lent, borrowed, speculated upon and invested. Finance capitalism monopolized this industry of capital as it circulated among the mega-corporations and coursed through the global banking system. With the assistance of complicit nation-states, profits rarely trickled down through corporate or capital gains taxes to fund the social welfare systems for dispossessed people. Those costs, meager as they may have been, could be paid for by taxes paid by working people, not the megaliths at the top.

With a war raging across the globe, anticolonial movements of workers and farmers like Gita's asked what this transition from industrial capitalism to finance capitalism meant for colonialism. At face value, their answer seemed simple: colonialism as they knew it was dead, but to bury it was not so easy. In finance capitalism, profits were seemingly airlifted from the workers' backs, an endless theft more invisible than Adam Smith's benign hand of the market. The market of finance capital never came to town to ply its wares, neither collateralized debt obligations nor leveraged buyout deals. It never bothered to make or sell anything of use to the populace. Finance capital saw no need for investment to build trade infrastructure or to maintain order by expensive military conquest in the colonies. The trickle-down grift of finance capitalism was debt combined with the one-way flight of capital to the old imperial centers. Imperial tribute, or colonies' payments to their sovereign, ended; but the ownership of key industries remained in the pockets of former colonizers, as did industry profits. One difference after colonialism: any old debts carried by previous imperial owners would be paid for by the newly independent nations. And the colonizers' banks, by and large, remained in new nations—sometimes side by side with national banks, sometimes with no competition at all. The circulation of capital passed through these old corridors of power, regardless of the change of flags and governance.

At local levels, the time-worn lenders' tricks of balloon interest rates and the promise of easy money to pay for basic needs only grew more essential to cover medicine, food, education and shelter. Workers and farmers competed with all the workers of the world for their wage rates and agricultural produce prices. Old collectivities of peasant and working-class survival sought to harness their techniques of shared-fund circles, one small-bore attempt to hold onto any and all means of production, whether plow, land, livestock, or loom. Revolution and the refusal to give up the lion's share of their work was another increasingly critical method. Gita Bandyopadhyay, as a member of the radical women's movement in Bengal and the Communist Party of India, faced old tragedies in a new context. One result was an upheaval in women's strategies for radical social transformation.

KOLKATA, INDIA, AND BUDAPEST, HUNGARY, 1948

In 1948, Kolkata was a city in foment that seeded revolt spilling beyond the confines of independent India to revolutionary movements across Asia. The World Federation of Democratic

Youth held their Asian convention in Kolkata in February. Students from Indonesia, Vietnam, Myanmar, and elsewhere demanded independence not just from colonial occupation, but from capitalism itself. The militant position held by Indonesian young people sprang from betrayal: their new republic faced bombing by the Dutch.[9] The experiences of the Vietnamese participants mirrored their own. Entrenched in an insurgency to regain their recently declared independence, Vietnamese delegates told the story of French colonial refusal to let go and the Euro-American henchmen that supported them.[10]

As a member of the Communist Party of India (CPI), Gita worked in two formations that sought to organize working-class women and men: the labor movement and the women's coalition MARS. In 1947, Gita met with members of the Women's International Democratic Federation who conducted a tour of India and Burma to better understand the effects of colonialism on women and children.[11] In addition, Gita worked with Lu Cui, a Chinese Communist Party member who also worked in the central offices of WIDF. Cui spent time in Kolkata in 1948 to solidify plans to hold the Asian Women's Conference in India. These plans failed because of the deep distrust by Nehru's Congress Party members who thought that another anti-colonial gathering would be too disturbing to the status quo.[12] The Security Control Office decided to open a file on the activities of the WIDF in response to their refusal to accept the Indian government's decision to refuse the conference and deny visas to all international participants. By March 1948, the Congress Party had banned the Communist Party of India. Leaders and party workers went underground, but continued to meet and organize. As in colonial times, jails became cells for organizing as much as confinement. Gita's connection to WIDF remained firm, and she took the direction of the CPI to send her to Paris to work for the WIDF central offices.

A year later, in 1949, MARS was also banned, in part due to its connections to the CPI, and its members moved into hiding. Regional and national leaders were imprisoned or driven underground, moving constantly from house to house to escape arrest. The rural movement integral to MARS's activism, called Tebhaga, was also on the government's watchlist. In the Tebhaga movement that emerged after India's independence in 1947, farmworkers and small-landholding peasant women and men sought basic human rights: fair land practices and an end to the feudal tributes of forced labor (*begar*) and the sexual control of rural women.[13] Violent police repression that included widespread rape of rural women sought to crush the uprising that united peasants and agricultural workers of all backgrounds, Muslims and Hindus, *adivasis* (indigenous peoples) and Dalits (oppressed castes).

The MARS, Bengal's member organization in WIDF, developed powerful strategies to organize the "*sarbahara*," or "those who've lost everything."[14] Gita was an early member of MARS, and sought to organize refugees from Partition who lived on the streets of Kolkata, as well as other encampments of dispossessed women, men, and children. Members of MARS mobilized mass public protests of women seeking redress on their own behalf. They built leadership at local and regional levels among the most oppressed women. They developed the signature petition to represent the numbers of women who supported their demands and give heft to cross-class campaigns. Perhaps most revolutionary of all, they listened to dispossessed women. Rural landless women and urban, resettled refugees from India's partition violence were two central bases for MARS's membership. Demands for affordable food, clothing, and housing combined with a focus on women's economic independence to imagine women's future independence from need. MARS propaganda—its songs, plays, pamphlets, and speeches—explained women's basic survival issues through an analysis of regional class conflict and capitalism's global imperial war.

Radical women developed powerful tools of protest during the British occupation of India and they further honed their methods during the early years of India's independence under the Congress Party. The story of Pratibha Ganguly and her comrades has the contours of their struggle archetype: the mass protest of women in public.[15] One afternoon in April 1949 the members of MARS gathered with their children in Kolkata. They used a technique they'd mobilized during the famine in 1942, one that forced the colonial government to address widespread hunger, homelessness, and unemployment. A large group of women marched peacefully in the public streets to government offices. Their demands in 1949 also mirrored their demands in 1942 when these mass protests of women had addressed the state: for civil liberties and livelihood support. They demanded the release of political prisoners, many of whom had been imprisoned without charges, and basic amenities of food, clothing, and work.

In 1942, they faced the British colonial government. In 1949, they addressed the ruling Congress Party government. This time, instead of beating, jailing, and roughly dispersing the women, as happened in 1942, the police fired on the protest and killed five people: four women and one child. Pratibha Ganguly was one of the women who died. The novelty of women's public protest shifted from a shocking sight of women filling the streets to a body count. Women protested their living conditions of impoverishment, and demanded their rights as citizens (not subjects) of India, and they were killed by the Indian police. After this police shooting, MARS was banned by the Congress government, and the women of MARS blended into their surroundings to carry on organizing in secret.

Gita took a slightly different route from many of her comrades, and flew as one of two Indian delegates to WIDF's Second Congress, held in Budapest, Hungary, in December, 1948. She didn't return to Kolkata until 1951. After the conference in Budapest, she traveled to Paris to work at the central offices of WIDF in Paris. Alongside the Secretary of WIDF from the People's Republic of China, Lu Cui, and the French communist Simone Bertrand, she shouldered much of the logistics, outreach, and communication for WIDF's mandate to support women's anti-colonial organizing. Lu Cui's work involved considerable travel to colonized regions of the world to develop WIDF's contacts with local organizers and support their activism. Between 1949 and 1951, Gita mostly traveled within Europe, with some notable exceptions. As her letters attest, she, quite literally in some cases, represented anti-colonial struggles around the world to internationalist allies.

PRIMITIVE ACCUMULATION

By the end of 1948, when Gita arrived, the central offices of the Women's International Democratic Federation had been running for three years. Its official membership was ninety- one million women. Located in Paris, the postwar global city for anti-fascist organizing, its staff enjoyed support from the pro-communist government. By 1950, France's central government had changed, and WIDF's welcome was worn thin. Eugenie Cotton, president of WIDF, also worked to found the World Peace Council. Eugenie was arrested for advocating that women should tear up their sons' enlistment papers to fight against the

Vietnamese liberation movement. As Adeline Broussan details in "Resistantes Against the Colonial Order," Vietnamese women radicalized French communist women through what she calls "grassroots diplomacy" at WIDF gatherings.[16] Their radicalization also galvanized the major shift within the French Communist Party to denounce French colonialism in absolute terms. But the consolidation of anti-colonialism at the French imperial center came with a cost. By January 1951, the WIDF offices moved to Berlin—the Berlin of the state-socialist German Democratic Republic, where they stayed until 1991.

"It seems they are quite the aristocracy over there in Berlin," Gita wrote on July 1, 1954.[17] This letter went to another staff member from these early years: Betty Millard, a communist party member in the United States, who had worked alongside her in Paris from 1949 to 1951. Gita worked as part of WIDF's Anticolonial International Preparatory Committee to support women's organizations in colonized regions of the world. Betty was an editor of the CPUSA journal *New Masses* for four years before arriving in Paris. Millard edited the English-language edition of WIDF's *Information Bulletin* that publicized international, regional, and national campaigns for women's emancipation. Like Gita, Betty also solidified international outreach by the organization, and gathered information about ongoing local campaigns of its member organizations for the *Bulletin* and solidarity campaigns.

"But we may be pleased to remember that we did the primitive accumulation part," Gita wrote. "Now we are again engaged in primitive accumulation."[18] Gita's primitive accumulation, along the grain of Rosa Luxemburg's use of the term, described the process of creating value from something in its raw, unrealized form. In jest, Gita flipped the term on its head. Rather than referring to the profits capitalism requires from commodifying non-capitalist land, resources, and labor, Gita imagined a communist primitive accumulation that built valuable revolutionary movements from scattered struggles against oppression. Left feminist activism that created movements in Budapest, Paris, Kolkata, Beijing, and New York, to name just a few locations, built the women's movement in these years.

While in Paris, Gita played a key role organizing the 1949 Asian Women's Conference. Her primitive accumulation plumbed the soil of internationalism after the destruction of a planetary war. They strengthened old values of common worth, not as a hidden ore below humanity's surface, but as an affirmed commonalty of vision and purpose. Even in the years when WIDF was welcome in Paris, this work was hardscrabble in the wreckage that a fascist war left behind: of broken lives, destroyed communities, betrayal and ongoing colonial occupation.

In 1950, Gita was part of the team that coordinated WIDF's first international campaign for peace in Korea. She attended campaign organizational meetings across Europe. Betty wrote press releases and speeches. WIDF framed the campaign in two ways. First, WIDF described women's activism as it forged a solidarity against US-led imperialist aggression, led by women from Korea, but also women from other colonized countries. Second, WIDF framed the campaign as a maternalist fight by all women from imperialist and colonized nations against the use of their sons and husbands as cannon fodder. The World Peace Council, co-founded in 1947 by WIDF members, joined their campaign against the attack on North Korea by US military forces, demanding peace, self-determination, and an end to American occupation of the region. They sought the support of the Chinese forces to help them in their fight against superior air power and chemical weapons that decimated whole populations. They framed American imperialism, not the North Korean government's attempt to break the Rhee government of South Korea by crossing the 38th parallel, as the defining trigger for war.

This framing remains contentious, since it overturns the current historical consensus about the instigation of the Korean War, as Bruce Cumings exhaustively details.[19] Yet, even in Cumings's careful untangling of which side's military forces acted first, the precipitating act of war is hard to locate with any certainty, nor with any clear gain in our understanding of the conflict. The perspective of delegates to the WIDF conferences included women from both south and north of the 38th parallel; as communists, they all shared their analysis in support of North Korea. Their perspective about the larger context of imperialist occupation refuted the dominant narrative that the US forces and the South Korean military had simply responded to North Korea's initiating an overture to war by launching their capture of territory far beyond the 38th parallel in June 1950.

The first UN-backed invasion began soon afterwards, when the United States launched a military response to the North Korean advance into the region designated as South Korea in the years after the withdrawal of Japanese occupation. In alliance with the South Korean government led by Syngman Rhee, US and NATO forces pummeled North Korea for the next three years. The alacrity of American support for the South Korean government surprised the North Korean military. The sheer force of the US government's support for South Korea was overwhelming, including military ships, airpower, troops, and military expertise. The early speed of North Korean forces in occupying parts of South Korea, including Seoul, was quickly halted and decisively pushed back by the end of 1950. At the end of the conflict, over three million Koreans were killed; it is estimated that at least two million were civilian deaths.[20] In North Korea alone, civilians were half of the two million people killed. Over these three years, American planes dropped 635,000 tons of bombs and 32,557 tons of napalm on the country. By 1952, no military targets remained, but the onslaught continued until 1953. The WIDF campaign against the Korean War spanned women's activism around the world to frame peace as a women's issue. In the words of historian Suzy Kim, "socialist internationalism in the context of a global peace movement facilitated a productive understanding of *difference*—whether gendered, racial, ethnic, national or any other—toward a 'transversal' politics of solidarity as seen during the Korean War."[21] Michelle Chase provides a fascinating account of Cuban women's dedicated solidarity to the global campaign against US military intervention in Korea. Chase focuses on Edith Buchaca, who attended the Asian Women's Conference in 1949, and Candelaria Rodríguez, a member of the WIDF fact-finding team that toured North Korean cities devastated by war. The solidarity of complicity that refused the conscription of soldiers from colonized countries to fight for imperialism shifted to what Chase calls "internationalist solidarity."[22] Internationalist solidarity refused to support the imperialist war machine; but it also articulated a prosocialist alternative to imperialism through anticolonial women's unity.

In 1951, Gita returned to India and the activism of the Mahila Atmaraksha Samiti. As she joked to Betty, their work of primitive accumulation in Paris gave organizational form to shared ideals and disparate contexts around the world. Organizing to build socialism, with women's equality and justice at the heart of this vision, simply continued after they returned to their countries of origin. Gita and Betty wrote to each other for decades after spending those two years in Paris building WIDF together. In no small part due to their countries' anti-communist clampdown, they never met again.

Gita's 1954 letter to Betty spurs two questions faced by most, but not all activists who were part of anti-imperialist internationalism during this period. How do you build a feminist people's movement for revolution grounded in a nation-state that doesn't want you there? And how do you build this movement alongside someone who's halfway around the world? Movement-building—or in Gita's creative reuse of Luxemburg's term, primitive accumulation—developed during the forties and fifties through WIDF's centrifugal energy of an international organization. The creativity and vitality did not come from the central offices in Paris, but from the varied struggles waged in colonized, post-colonial, and imperial contexts. International organizations like WIDF meant little without the bullets taken by its members, and the campaigns launched by its affiliated women's groups that they won and lost and won again.

BUDAPEST, HUNGARY, 1948, AND BEIJING, PEOPLE'S REPUBLIC OF CHINA, 1949

Gita and Betty first met in 1948 at WIDF's Second International Women's Congress, held in Budapest, Hungary. The Congress in Budapest brought members to assess their activism since founding three years earlier. The decision to focus on women's anti-colonial activism in 1946 expanded their founding commitment to anti-fascism.[23] WIDF explicitly added anti-racism and anti-colonialism to its commitment to fighting fascism. Women from the US delegation and women from the Indian, Vietnamese, Moroccan, Algerian, and Chinese delegations sought this clarity from WIDF's inception. They gained solidarity for their demand from African American activists who made sure anti-racism was another explicit goal. In this sense, they adhered to a definition of fascism honed in the 1930s.

Marxist theorist R. Palme Dutt, a member of the Communist Party of Great Britain, defined fascism as an integral ideology of capitalism since it was the defense of last resort. Fascism maintained capitalism in the face of revolutionary upheaval. It intensified the dictatorship of capitalism and the repression of the working class. Fascism also concentrated each imperialist block into a single economic and political unity. War only solidified the antagonisms and contradictions within imperialism. Dutt also characterized fascism as a movement through its actors: "Fascism, in short, is a movement of mixed elements dominantly petit bourgeois, but also slum proletarian and demoralized working class, financed and directed by finance capital, by the big industrialists, landlords and financiers, to defeat the working-class revolution and smash the working class organization."[24] What made fascism specific, in Dutt's analysis, was its reliance on overt violence and illegal methods to shore up the capitalist system in crisis.

WIDF members from around the world sharpened a gendered and racialized analysis of fascism during these heady years from 1945 to the mid-1950s. They mobilized women's socially-dominant role as mothers and maternalist rhetoric to attack fascism. But anti-fascism in their publications also emphasized women's willingness to fight, physically and militarily, against fascist violence. WIDF's public materials used the terms of maternalism not as a biological destiny, but as a social role that anti-fascist, anti-racist, and anti-colonial women shaped rather than simply inhabited.

Gita contributed to the central document presented at the 1948 conference, "The Women of Asia and Africa." The report began with a quotation from the United Nations Charter's Article 73 about "non-self-governing territories" that affirmed "that the interests of the inhabitants of these territories are paramount, and [we] accept as a sacred trust the obligation to promote to the utmost, within the system of international peace and security established by the present Charter, the well-being of the inhabitants of these territories," with cultural rights and self-government upheld.[25] The photo the WIDF included after this passage showed the severed heads of anti-colonial insurgents on stakes. Underneath was the caption, "Here is how the colonialist countries respect the charter of the United Nations which they signed."[26]

As a member working in the WIDF's central offices in Paris, Gita was on the Asian Women's Conference organizing committee. She spent over a month in China beforehand to prepare for the gathering. She also attended as a delegate. Due to the hostile political climate in India, she used a pseudonym, Mira Mitra, for her speech about children's conditions in India.

PARIS, FRANCE, AND WARSAW,
POLAND, 1950–1951

Gita and Betty became close while working together in Paris. They shared a wry sense of humor and a keen eye for the absurd. The two attended the WIDF executive committee meetings in Berlin held in February, 1951, where they decided to send an investigative team to Korea.

On March 5, 1951, Gita wrote to Betty about a train journey she took after the meetings with the East German contingent from Berlin, GDR, to Warsaw, Poland, to attend a WIDF-spon-

Figure 6. Gita Bandyopadhyay and Betty Millard (dressed in pants and shirts) and Marie Jeusse, Juliette Dubois, Genevieve Denis, and Germaine Huby-Gosselin (wearing saris), Weissensee, outside Berlin, May 6, 1951. Photo courtesy of Sophia Smith Archives, Smith College.

sored rally for peace as part of the "Hands Off Korea" campaign. Gita was sure her adventure would make Betty "green with envy" as she sat in Paris editing the *Bulletin Anglais:*

> I never knew the German women possessed as loud voices as the Bengalis and Americans or could speed up their speech like the French. Four of those German women—extremely friendly and delightful—four among the 91 million front ranks, kept up a nonstop conversation for 4 hours while the rather bewildered Bengali—also a front member of a more colonial order tried to catch a bit of sleep.... At the stroke of twelve, suddenly the noise increased a thousandfold and in spite of the gradually developing deafness of the Bengali type, her eardrums seemed to be on the bursting point![27]

Gita's inability to rest on the overnight journey was compounded when five men entered the compartment carrying bottles of vodka to jumpstart a party.

> Peeping through a buttonhole, I beheld the following spectacle: in front of me (the compartment by the way, was 6 × 3 feet in size) a pug-nosed, bald-headed, perpetually smiling man; next to him one of the 91 millions [a member of WIDF], squeezed like a tomato in a sandwich; next, another stub-nosed, toothbrush-moustache, bald-headed Pole holding a vodka bottle near Elli's [Schmidt, President of the Democratic Union of German Women] unwilling mouth.... They pushed me and thrust the vodka bottle to my horrified mouth, making me reflect a little bit on the inferiority of the European civilization!! I shouted "Dormir" in pure French because I couldn't really remember any other language and shut my eyes as tightly as possible. In a little while the room became dead quiet and a load fell on my side. "Hai ah" I shouted and found this giant, bald-head sleeping comfortably on my side smelling of vodka and on hearing me shout punched me affectionately!

The train journey ended with Gita's glasses broken after wrestling to avoid a hug.

> On arriving, one of the toothbrush types thought of making up with an Asiatic type by asking for my Mao Tse Tung badge, which I immediately gave him, fearing being vodka sprinkled. With the greatest passion he threw his arms around me and in the process of his trying to launch a toothbrush kiss and me trying to avoid it, a "crack" was heard leaving my spectacles a little damaged which resulted in the blindness of my right eye.... Well, Bettuska, would you ever again travel by plane? I would never. Life would be much uninteresting in contrast in such 12 hours—wouldn't it?!!

Bandyopadhyay's racialization of her journey multiplied and refracted through her telling: to be a "Bengali type" sent up ethnic codes of regionalized India. These regional types are colonial, since they were constructed and mobilized in the divide-and-conquer techniques honed by the British, as well as national, since they continued to have characteristic typecasting within

India after independence. The "Asiatic type" she references carries a racism that crosses the globe and does not rely on overt colonialism for its violence. "European civilization," while intrinsic to the colonial rationalization of manifest destiny, in Bandyopadhyay's story is synonymous with the alcoholic sexual harassment endemic to colonizing countries.

The cacophony of languages, with exclamations in French and Hindi embedded in German, Polish, and English, adds yet another layer of humor through discomfort. Her final riposte, of always traveling by train, never plane, embeds a class analysis in her tale. The bourgeois manners of plane travel would have shut down the possibility of mayhem altogether. The humor of Gita's storytelling relied upon a critique of colonialism and male supremacism that she shared with the letter's recipient, without a doubt. But her humorous indirection also relied on a deeper level of intimacy, one of shared sensibility and knowledge that the humor in its anti-imperialist complexity would be understood.

HANDS OFF KOREA CAMPAIGN, 1950–1953

With Gita's vision blurred in her right eye and a perpetual wink to gain some vision in her left eye, the Congress for Peace began. The international peace movement against the bombing of Korea by US forces was the central topic. Gita described her role as one "of a more colonial order" through the parochial but deeply felt solidarity of WIDF's Polish delegates:

> In the meantime, all the Polish women present at the Congress wanted me to be a Korean. This led to many tears and embraces, very touching, but it left me a bit shy on account of taking all the courageous fight of the Koreans on me.[28]

This was not Gita's first experience with this form of parochial solidarity. A year earlier Gita added a personal note to Betty that she attached to a WIDF report she wrote from Budapest, Hungary.

> You may call me an imposter or whatever you like but the fact is that the Hungarians insist on my being a Korean and I like it or not I am a Korean in Budapest. But thanks to the People's government I have not yet encountered the inevitable questions in regard to jungles—snakes and tigers. It is wonderful to see how much they are propagating for Korea. Everywhere, in streets, in colleges, in cinemas one would find "HANDS OFF KOREA" posters. I wish Pak Den Ai [Pak Chŏng-ae] and the other Korean comrades could see all of this.[29]

Betty wrote to her mother about meeting Pak Chŏng-ae, a committed anti-colonial leader in North Korea who was the chair of the Democratic Women's Union of Korea and served on the WIDF Executive Council since 1948. Like Gita, she used the transliteration used in WIDF documents during this period. "I have a Korean friend, Pak Den Ai, when I first met her in Budapest we could only smile and shake hands and talk sign language—by the time we met in Peking [Beijing] I had learned a few words of Russian and she of English—now in Helsinki we know a little more and we're old friends."[30] They first met in Budapest at WIDF's Second International Congress, then renewed their friendship on the train from Moscow on their way to the Asian Women's Conference the following year, and met again at the Executive Council meetings in Helsinki in 1950 after the Korean War had begun.

By 1951, these interpersonal linkages smoothed the campaign to oppose the US military campaign against Korea. At the invitation of Pak Chŏng-ae and the Korean Women's Democratic League, a WIDF fact-finding delegation of twenty-one women

To Save the World / 137

Figure 7. Pak Chŏng-ae attending the Asian Women's Conference, Beijing, December 1949. Photo courtesy of Sophia Smith Archives, Smith College.

from eighteen countries traveled to North Korea in May 1951 to witness the carpet bombing and ground troop assault. They filmed what they saw and the women they met, yet another proof of the veracity of their claims. Their report, *We Accuse!*, was issued in five languages: English, French, Russian, Chinese, and Korean. As the campaign rippled outward, it was translated into twenty languages.[31] *We Accuse!* galvanized women's organizations around the world to oppose the US military occupation of Korea. It also spurred the United States to hold congressional hearings to refute their findings, particularly about the use of chemical warfare on civilian populations, an act of human rights abuse against the Geneva conventions.

WIDF's report detailed with devastating specificity how American and UN forces tortured eleven-year-old girls, buried the people of entire villages alive, and raped women until they died. They submitted their report, with its graphic and well-documented testimony of chemical and biological warfare, to the United Nations. As a result of their opposition to the Korean War, as Taewoo Kim describes, they lost their consultative status to the UN Economic and Social Council, a status not returned until 1967.[32] Some of the women who visited war sites, spoke to women, and wrote the report lost their jobs or faced other retribution such as imprisonment, but no one recanted the truth of their findings.[33] *We Accuse* fueled the global peace campaign to rally against the atrocities by United States and NATO troops committed in Korea. Michelle Chase characterizes the activism by two Cuban revolutionary women in this international campaign, Edith García Buchaca, who attended the Asian Women's Conference, and another, Candelaria Rodríguez, who traveled to Korea as part of WIDF's fact-finding mission.

> Their combined stories suggest that some Cuban women found inspiration and meaning in global struggles for women's emancipation and that they saw these as linked to broader questions of national liberation, decolonization, and socialist revolution. Finally, their conceptual framework helps explain why women's anti-war activism in this period was not restricted to maternalist references to women's natural desire for peace.[34]

"Hands Off Korea!" read the posters on the streets of Hungary and Poland. "Germany No Second Korea!" was one slogan in East Germany. Another poster was more visceral: "Vermin Infestation. Korea is a warning! Fight for peace against the criminals of humanity."[35] Giant fleas with the faces of Truman, Churchill, and Adenauer crawled toward the poster's viewer. The name of the campaign in the Soviet Union was "Struggle for Peace!" In the United States, American Women for Peace, with Betty

Millard playing a central coordinating role, launched the antiwar "Save Our Sons!" campaign. Chase describes the solidarity campaign in Cuba, where the Democratic Federation of Cuban Women poured their energy into the campaign. A flyer read, "Imperialists Demand Cuban Blood! Let's Save Our Children!"[36] Millions of signatures were collected on petitions against the Korean War around the world. American women launched a letter-writing campaign to President Truman demanding the release of WIDF's report to the American public.[37]

International Women's Day became the touchpoint for anti-imperialism in the US leftist women's movement beginning in 1950, as these women heeded the call for solidarity issued by the Asian Women's Conference. By contrast, Gita's organization revived International Women's Day within India even earlier, in 1943. Claudia Jones, the chair of the CPUSA Women's Commission, and a close comrade of Betty Millard, wrote numerous articles against the bombardment of Korea in her column "Half the World" in the *Daily Worker*. The US government arrested her three times between 1950 and 1951 under the Smith Act (the Alien Registration Act) and the McCarren Act, which required communist organizations to register with the US Attorney General. Her speech "International Women's Day and the Struggle for Peace" was the reason for her first arrest.[38] As part of an upsurge in active refusal of government foreign policy and domestic priorities, Jones was truly part of a global moment in history. In Syria, the two delegates who attended the Asian Women's Conference, Amine Aref Hasan and Salma Boummi, were also arrested for leading an International Women's Day protest against the government.

In 1953, Claudia Jones contested her imprisonment to a US court:

> Will you measure, for example, as worthy of one year's sentence, my passionate adherence to the idea of fighting for full unequivocal equality for my people, the Negro people, which as a Communist I believe can only be achieved allied to the cause of the working class? A year for another vital Communist belief that the bestial Korean war is an unjust war? Or my belief that peaceful coexistence can be achieved and peace won if struggled for?[39]

Internationalism during this period was a praxis that had two terrains, one imperialist and the other under imperial domination. Both espoused shared ideals and picked a fight. This praxis asked every activist to choose a side: in favor of imperialist occupation and war, or against.

BUDGE BUDGE, SOUTH 24 PARGANAS, 1951

Gita returned to a vastly different nation in 1951. The communist party was no longer underground. Women energized by struggles in the 1940s gained some victories in the 1950s. When they fought alongside peasant men during the much-celebrated Tebhaga movement, they began with a demand for more grain from their harvest. They then pursued their rights to the land they sowed. Peasant women activists joined the communist party and peasant organizations linked to the communists. They made manifest demands that communists before them may have heard, but let wait for another day. Peasant women demanded an end to the interpersonal violence that structured their pinched horizons. Gargi Chakravartty described the direct criticisms of the CPI lodged by members of MARS in 1952:

> At a meeting, sometime in November 1952, Communist women discussed threadbare, the politburo's document on 'Task on the Women's Front.' While appreciating the call for a separate broad-

based, multi-class organization of women for equal rights, they disagreed with the Party for not addressing the issue of the 'double yoke of oppression.' They expressed their resentment that the Party document had failed to link the social with the economic demands of women. They were critical about the Party's formulations regarding working-class women as they did not address gender inequality.[40]

As Chakravartty wrote, organized peasant women added another dimension of patriarchal violence into the frontlines of communist struggles. Violence was not entirely at the hand of the state, they said, but also embedded itself in the patriarchal relations that gave husbands and parents-in-law control over the movement and actions of women. Additionally, peasant women successfully argued they should have the right to their own earnings unconditionally. Land to those who worked on it. Fruits of labor to the worker. If the peasant family was the only unit to measure justice, then peasant women working every day of their lives would see little of it. Women's rights within these families, they argued, required enumeration, attention, and organization woven into communist mores. These lessons came from struggles that had heavy costs.

Yet Gita also returned to a nation where little had changed since 1948. Even with communists living above ground, they faced unending harassment from the police. Communist women fighting for basic justice issues for the most vulnerable people in their localities faced more subtle, but just as wrenching pressures. The social boycott was one popular velvet hammer wielded against women activists, for daring to move more freely in and out of homes, for demanding an audience at the local police stations, for listening to women's stories, and for addressing groups in public places. The old trope of honor as a cudgel used against women placed suspicion on their service. These whisper campaigns jeopardized these women's ability to buy food from local merchants, or kerosene for their stoves, or any of the other small necessities of life. Gossip and personal slander that impugned their morality were a nuisance. Social boycotts, however, could mean expulsion from a neighborhood and disruption of movement building.

Gita moved to the rural heartland of militant jute mill workers, an area called Budge Budge in South 24 Parganas, and plunged into peasant and workers' struggles through organizing rural women. Upper-caste, college-educated organizers like Gita learned the lives of the rural poor by living alongside the rural poor. Their choices were not temporary ones. They did not spend a little time in one place before moving to another. Brahmin caste status was largely lost in the process, since the work and contact with the rural poor of diverse caste and religious backgrounds had cultural consequences. Gita's comrade Pratibha Ganguly had been a beloved communist organizer in Budge Budge, trudging daily through the marshy ground of rural localities even during heavy monsoon rains to talk with peasant women. Between 1947 and 1951, eleven thousand peasants and activists had been arrested in South 24 Parganas alone.[41] When Ganguly was killed by the police in the women's march for peace and rights in 1949, she left tracks and networks that Bandyopadhyay followed.

Every day of her work in Budge Budge held long-standing difficulties. Health issues—of simple dysentery and endemic malaria—were life-threatening when food and basic medicines, even topical antibiotics, were so scarce. In her letters to Betty Millard, Gita described the need for quinine, or thanked Betty for the latest supplies sent. She organized along the grain of communist tradition: provide relief for daily needs and build the means for women to determine their own demands. With one other woman from South 24 Parganas, Bandyopadhyay opened a school in Ganguly's name for women and girls. At first the school failed, since both the Muslim and Hindu women in the area said they were too busy to attend. They did not think that the school met their needs. Even after scouring the region, only two women joined the school. In response, they developed specialized outreach methods for women of different ages: literacy for girls and young women, skilled work like midwifery, sewing, and handicrafts for women in midlife, and organizing training for older women whose children had grown.

By 1953, the school had gained the enthusiasm of women, young and old, who enrolled their daughters. Older women used their organizing skills to open new MARS chapters across the region. Middle-aged women opened women's work cooperatives and schools. Young women created groups for teen girls (*Kishore bahinis*). The membership of MARS burgeoned in West Bengal through the proliferation of schools, job-training sites, and self-help initiatives. They still fought for women's right to live free from violence. They still confronted the state for its neglect. But they also built the strength of women to live independently in the process. Bandyopadhyay's school in Budge Budge became a model for radical women's education and proliferated across West Bengal.

INTERNATIONALISM

The train journey from Berlin to Warsaw returned in Gita's letters, this time through the lens of nostalgia. In her first letter to Betty after landing in Kolkata, she announced her sudden

Figure 8. Gita Bandyopadhyay and Subhash Mukhopadhyay, undated. Photo courtesy of Sophia Smith Archives, Smith College.

marriage to a well-known revolutionary poet and communist, Subhash Mukhopadhyay. "I am so anxious to know your reactions on this. Subhash (my husband) felt a bit jealous of you when I told him how all of you kissed me on all occasions and even men with moustaches embraced me."[42]

The love within the movement, and its showering of affection, wanted and undesired, stayed uppermost in Gita's memories of this time. She also returned to what she calls the glamour of WIDF. Gita's passport was seized by the government as soon as she returned—as was Betty's in the United States. In 1953 she wrote to Betty during WIDF's Third International Women's Congress, held in Copenhagen, Denmark. Neither could attend, but each of their national delegations at the massive women's conference was large and enthusiastic:

I feel a pang near my heart remembering the good old days. Remember being photographed in Berlin every two minutes? Imagine the Congress in Denmark. Click, click—click, click—the cameras go. I am here in this remote jungle in a hut beside a ditch. You are somewhere in Latin America may be.[43]

Internationalism is a lofty invocation. Unlike imperialism, with the class-targeted hardships of scarcity, it's harder to see the increments of international solidarity: of relationships, affection, laughter and shared ideals. As Rachel Leow and Su Lin Lewis emphasize in their scholarship about activism in Asia during the early and mid-1950s, even in avowedly leftist spaces, the visions for socialism were wide-ranging, fluid, and under construction by Asian activists across the region.[44] It's also difficult to imagine how to put solidarity with women across the globe into practice. In West Bengal, in 1953, leftist women distributed petitions for peace across the state and collected thousands of signatures. These were symbolic gestures against the Korean War, against ongoing colonial occupation and counter-insurgency. But each signature by a rural woman had education behind it: discussions about the struggles for anti-imperialist peace and the fights waged by women against imperialism around the world. Each signature was also a celebration of the fight for literacy won by that woman. Each signature provided a material record of her place in this wider collectivity that dared to imagine what the world could be.

Conclusion

The Asian Women's Conference provided an early clarion call for methods to combine older lessons of socialist activism against European extractive and settler colonialism with the new context of US financial imperialism. Participants represented movements that organized the masses of people where they lived. But organizing the masses to fight the colonial occupation of land and its wealth could not counter the nimbler form of US imperialism that emerged in 1945. This colonial form, sometimes called neocolonialism, sought land footprints for military bases rather than overt conquest and occupation. Postwar US imperialism gained a monopoly over the global financial system, and weaponized financial systems in even more effective ways than the settler or extractive colonial forms that preceded it. This imperialism cemented global financial dominance with mushrooming US military outposts, gained through newly-independent nations' complicit governments rather than territorial occupation.

The praxis developed by the women from Vietnam, Indonesia, India, Malaysia, and China did not mirror the spreading hopscotch of military bases that marked the imperialism of US finance. This praxis still centered rural people's issues at the heart of their vision for equality. This praxis still focused on the most exploitative, most oppressive relations of marginalized women's lives, needs, and desires. This praxis against patriarchy and against capitalism knit a socialism that linked those rural women's issues of survival to an internationalist refusal to be co-opted through the financial straightjackets of imperial-controlled banking systems, imperial-owned debt, and US-backed federal reserves.

Celestine Ouezzin Coulibaly, whose speech at Beijing opened this book, was one of the founders and the secretary of the RDA, a communist-allied political organization that spanned French colonies across West and Equatorial Africa. She also built the Abidjan Women's Committee, with ten thousand members. During the conference in Beijing, she stressed the importance of organizing dispossessed rural and urban women as vital to the anti-colonial movement she led. She described a powerful struggle in Bobo Dioulasso, a large city in what was then Upper Volta and now is Burkina Faso, when the women opposed polygamy:

> They went to the Administrator for his authorization to return to their own families, but he kept them prisoner to oblige them to go back to their husbands' establishments. They were made to pull up the fine grass in front of the Court House all day long under the hot sun. Corporal punishment and starvation were employed. But as the news went round, the number of women who came to be made prisoner increased. The Administrator was afraid, and was obliged to free all of these women.[1]

These specific struggles provide insight about the temperature of women's activism, about the techniques that worked, and about the locations for victory. Her story also reminded her audience of women's struggles against cultural practices like polygamy that powerfully shaped their lives under colonialism. Women organized by Coulibaly and many others opposed the cultural hegemony of polygamy from within their own communities. They also defied the colonial regimes that cemented these traditions as laws. The women from Bobo Dioulasso won their fight against the local administrator because they had the numbers, they were not afraid of colonial punishments, they had community support, and they were united in their goals. The lesson of her story is plainly drawn: the successful fight for women's rights to full humanity unraveled the fabric that held imperialism in place. Women could not be additions to anti-imperialist struggle if the movement for socialism sought to win. Coulibaly traveled the length and breadth of West Africa to address groups of women after the Asian Women's Conference. She challenged the women as well as the men to have the courage for the necessary struggle to emancipate women as an integral part of their shared anti-imperialist fight.

Revolutionary movements in Vietnam and in China, as well as in Burkina Faso, Ghana, Tanzania, Angola, and elsewhere on the African and Asian continents did not forget the organizing methods voiced at the Women's International Democratic Federation conferences during the 1940s and 1950s. These movements also listened to the voices of the people, and built alternatives to imperial financial occupation. For decades, they maintained solidarity across disparate locations. The Women's Bureau of the Afro-Asian People's Solidarity Organization (AAPSO) originated in the early sixties and met regularly for the next two decades. In preparation for the UN Conference on Women held in Nairobi, Kenya in 1985, the AAPSO Presidium Committee on Women members met numerous times to shape their demands.² They sought to put imperialism on the agenda as a women's issue, and led women from Europe to support resolutions that denounced the occupation of Palestine and the apartheid state of South Africa.³ The inside/outside organizing strategy for women's internationalism continued well after the Asian Women's Conference faded from memory. We can still hear this strategy as a lament about women's lost political consciousness about imperialism, an amnesia afflicting women from within imperial nations. In the twenty-first century, Pakistani socialist feminist and founder of the Women's Action Forum Nighat Said Khan framed this vision for a more transformational transnational feminist movement. "We in the South can do our best but until the women's movement and feminist academics in the North are also against their respective states and the international world order, we will never see a global women's movement."⁴ Khan articulates the vision of this other anticolonial and socialist feminism that exists in our current moment as well.

Transnational feminism, as we now call women's movements that cross nation-state borders (sometimes along official state-sanctioned connections and sometimes against or beyond those linkages), was not fated to follow the United Nations model after the close of the Second World War. In the UN model, women's issues are funneled through nominally independent nation-states alongside satellite non-governmental feminist organizations that can advocate for issues, but neither shape a political party nor stand for elections. Transnational feminist movements have hit a wall: the nonprofit industrial complex renders feminist activism all but toothless in the face of powerful moneyed and geopolitical interests. The critique of our current moment is annihilating, with seemingly few options for systemic change. But possible answers remain in circulation.

The reconstructive work to flesh out our collective memory about an anti-imperialist transnational feminist vision is daunting in the face of the stubborn innocence of many women's movements that inhabit the wealthy nations made rich by colonialism and trafficking in the people captured in transatlantic slavery. These afterlives of violence demand recognition. Khan's analysis draws from the legacy of women's internationalism that refused the comfort of innocence about imperial power and its attendant charity imbued with pitying maternalism. Khan envisioned a transnational women's movement as one built of women's differential relationships because of the geo-political power of dominant nation states in Europe and North America, but not determined by them. Women's common interests lay in the fight for a better world, one neither capitalist nor patriarchal, but grounded in women's emancipation as an integral part of the freedom of the world's oppressed people.

Leftist anticolonial women's movements, movements led by rural and urban poor and middle-class women, had another vision. By the mid-twentieth century, the pro-socialist women of militant anticolonial movements shaped a clear and compelling strategy for internationalism that percolated throughout the women's movement on the communist left. Its terms were militant and it advocated the violent overthrow of colonialism in Asia and Africa. Its analysis was geopolitically sensitive, since women in the pro-socialist West had a different role from women in the pro-socialist Third World, and different still from the communist bloc of the Soviet-aligned East.

For a period in the 1940s through the 1960s, the anti-colonial theory of internationalism shaped the terms of mutual assistance among women of the world. Humanitarian assistance falsely presumes the innocence of the givers—whether the innocence of nation-state's foreign policies or the innocence of well-meaning, wealthy donors. Rather than seeking allies or benefactors, this pro-socialist transnational feminism sought accomplices in struggle, since, they argued, no one exists on the sidelines of imperialism. Rather than humanitarian hand-outs, this anticolonial movement for a transformative feminism across the globe asked women to choose the arc of justice where all women, particularly the most marginalized, could shape their own destinies.

ACKNOWLEDGMENTS

Hajrah Begum's oral history in the Teen Murti archives in New Delhi first introduced me to the Women's International Democratic Federation (WIDF). She told a funny story about the contingent of Indian women who landed in Copenhagen in 1953 to attend WIDF's third Women's Congress. All of Copenhagen, it seemed to her, noticed their presence. The leadership of WIDF was thrilled at their visibility and commended them on bringing the attention of the working people of Denmark to their international conference of women. Intrigued, I next visited the women's history archives of Atria in Amsterdam and happened to run into Francisca de Haan as I read the *Information Bulletin* with growing interest. She fed my curiosity with her findings about WIDF's origins, as well as its ongoing mysteries of lost records from the late 1940s and early 1950s. By the time I interviewed Primula Loomba, a communist leader in the National Federation of Indian Women who had worked at WIDF's Berlin central office in the 1960s, I was hooked.

In 2019, myself and two scholars of socialist feminism, Wang Zheng and Kristen Ghodsee, gathered scholars from around the world who worked on socialist women and WIDF for the Global Socialist Feminism symposium at the University of Michigan. The joy of this gathering, which included Supriya Chotani, Michelle Chase, Katherine

Marino, Anup Grewal, Chiara Bonfiglioli, Francisca de Haan, and Abdelkadar Berrahmoun, still resonates in the relative stillness of pandemic-era scholarly collaboration. The generosity of archivists, scholars, activists, colleagues, students, friends and family still astounds me. Caty Seger handled most of the note-taking, archival collection and organizational work with care and foresight. Jodie Evans, a tireless anti-war and revolutionary feminist activist who co-founded Code Pink, believes that our twentieth-century excavation matters to anti-imperialist women's movements now, and her support for this conference made it possible. Without their collective wisdom, this project would be very different, with only the wisps of insight gleaned from the relatively scant written and visual records that remain of this international gathering of revolutionary and reforming women, who stretched across the globe by their hard daily work and visionary aspirations.

The omissions and errors of this story are mine, but the laughter and the care imbued throughout this complicated history of an international women's movement for socialism reflect the stories I've heard and the story I've lived. Students at Smith College and at the American University of Beirut translated materials from Arabic to English, French to English, and Spanish to English. Special thanks to Preetilata Hashemi, who traced the longer twentieth-century history of the Asian Women's Conference early in the project; to Caty Seger, who visited the Tamiment Archives in New York City more than once to find WIDF's official report on the US military atrocities during the Korean War; and to Vidya Yin and Ruoyu Zhang who worked on the final stage of the manuscript. Dr. Adeline Broussan was an active partner in this work, most memorably when she found the lost boxes of archives in Paris that shaped her own dissertation on the WIDF in Vietnam and France.

Kaoukab Chebaro at the AUB archives shared not only posters, letters, and meeting materials of women activists from Lebanon, Jordan, Palestine and Syria. She also found the people who could share even more about Lebanese and Syrian women's struggles for justice. I am still grateful to the archivists at the Sophia Smith archives at Smith College, only yards from my office, who quickly processed the records of Betty Millard, the US communist party member. Perhaps this should remain a secret, but thank you to Maida Goodwin at SSC who allowed me to sift through the materials even before they had been fully processed. Hala Dimechkie, a brilliant friend, shared her MA thesis about her activist grandmother, Julia Tu'Mi Dimashqiyi, as this project had just taken root. Hala's grandmother's story is here too: another layer of courageous defiance beneath these words.

Su Lin Lewis and Carolien Stolte, the editors of a forthcoming volume with University of Leiden Press, *The Lives of Cold War Afro-Asianism*, hosted zoom gatherings for collective sharing of our essays about experiments and collaborations that spanned the continents of Africa and Asia, but also Latin America and the Caribbean. Those lively conversations, with Su Lin, Wildan Sena Utama, and Taomo Zhou particularly, exceeded the task at hand to provide that wider lens of why these histories are so vital and also so fragile in our present time. They elaborated why these histories resuscitate hope that finance capital does not pull every lever of our worlds, and that the seeds of other possibilities are never fully dormant. I would also like to thank Alina Sajed and Sara Salem, the editors of a special issue of *Kohl: A Journal for Gender and Body Research* on anti-colonial feminist imaginaries, for their insights about this work.

With wisdom and sharp analytic editing, my friend and colleague Daphne Lamothe read more drafts than I can count and gave me bracing encouragement when I needed it most. Sujani Reddy, Jennifer Guglielmo, Michelle Joffroy, Darcy Buerkle, Ginetta Candelario, Sonya Meyerson-Knox, Dahlia Gubara, Ali Wick, Yemi Tessema, Laleh Khalidi, Nadya Sabaiti, Ghiwa Sayegh, Miriam Neptune, Liz Pryor, Jennifer DeClue, Mehammed Mack, Payal Banerjee, Kelly Anderson, Brooke Atherton, Rayan El-Amin, Alex Lubin, Kelly Gallagher, Dawn Peterson, Susannah Howe, Arianne Shahvisi, Neil Singh, Roula Seghaier, Nadje Al-Ali, Kiran Asher, Shailja Patel, Angie Willey, Vijay Prashad, Ziu Lifeng, Sudhanva Deshpande, Mala Hashmi, Asha Nadkarni, Jina Kim, and Manu Karuka patiently listened to more stories than I can remember. More than simply listening, they helped to shape the kernels of these stories, reminding me why I shouldn't let them go. For longstanding support in all things that matter, Githa Hariharan, U. Vasuki, Indu Agnihotri, Ruth Wilson

Gilmore, Himani Bannerji, Paula Giddings, Vicky Spelman, and Rajni Palriwala are foremost in my mind.

Layan Fuleiyan, Claudia De La Cruz, and Mikaela Erskog, comrades from the People's Forum, debated the finer points of revolutionary feminism of the past to sharpen our praxis today. My heartfelt appreciation goes to the activist-scholars of the feminist collective in the Tricontinental Institute for Social Research, especially Renata Porto Bugni, Satarupa Chakraborty, Ingrid Neves, Nontobeko Hlela, and Srujana Bodapati, who collaborated on the history of Kanak Mukherjee, the communist women's activist from Bengal. Suchetana Chattopadhyay read and shared drafts with especial care, in ways that opened the memories of close friends of Gita Bandyopadhyay at a time when we could not travel to share these memories in person.

Mary Hawkesworth published my earliest essay on this topic, "Before Bandung: The Anti-Imperialist Women's Movement in Asia and the Women's International Democratic Federation," *Signs* 41, no. 2 (Winter 2016): 305–31. Laura Briggs and Ginetta Candelario both gave invaluable editorial comments on a much later essay, "Peace and the Barrel of the Gun in the Internationalist Women's Movement, 1945–49," *Meridians: Feminism, Race, Transnationalism* 18, no. 2 (October 2019): 261–77. An early version of chapter 4 was published as "Gita, Betty and the Women's Democratic International Federation: An Internationalist Love Story," in *Faith in the Masses*, ed. Tony Pekinovsky (New York: International Publishers, 2020), 313–36. Also, parts of another essay are embedded in this book: "Indian Peasant Women's Activism in a Hot Cold War," in *Communist Histories, Vol. 1*, ed. Vijay Prashad (New Delhi: Leftword Books, 2016) and in *Gender, Sexuality and the Cold War: A Global Perspective*, ed. Philip E. Muehlenbeck (Nashville, TN: Vanderbilt University Press, 2017), 113–37. Finally, thanks to Niels Hooper and Naja Pulliam Collins at the University of California Press, who saw the promise in a rough manuscript and gave valuable advice at the right moments.

Being knee deep in the narrative is only one of many debts of gratitude. For Rosa and Zalia, courageous young people who dare to look and also see; who see, but also know where the silliest laughter lies. Thank you both for giving me the jump on every day. To my family during these years of subtle and cataclysmic changes: I am thankful to be together without divisions. To my movement elders, Brinda Karat and Subhashini Ali: every conversation, whether sunk in armchairs, raising our voices at a rally, or traversing the parks of Delhi and Kanpur, is embedded in these pages. Joelle Fishman, my comrade in New Haven, Connecticut, elaborated the metaphor of the dove in struggle for me decades ago; one wing is revolutionary patience, the other revolutionary action. Art Perlo enacted both of these qualities throughout his life, and he is missed but not gone.

NOTES

INTRODUCTION

1. Henriette Diabate, *La Marche des Femmes sur Grand-Bassam* (Abidjan: Nouvelles Editions Africaines, 1975): 21.
2. "To Our Sisters, the Women of the Countries of Asia," *Information Bulletin* 4, no. 7 (1950): 9, The Left Federation of Swedish Women, Swedish Labor Movement Archives, Huddinge, Sweden. Hereafter, Left Federation of Swedish Women.
3. "To Our Sisters, the Women of the Countries of Asia," 9.
4. China 1950 Diary, Box 17, Eslanda Goode Robeson Collection, Moorland-Springarn Research Center, Howard University, Washington, DC. Hereafter, Eslanda Goode Robeson Collection.
5. There are notable exceptions to this invisibility, including stellar dissertations and book-length examples listed in the Sources and Further Reading.
6. Betty Millard Collection, Sophia Smith Collection of Women's History, Smith College, hereafter Millard Collection, SSC.
7. Letter from Gita Bandyopadhyay to Betty Millard, Budapest, September 4, 1950, Millard Collection, SSC.
8. Accessible places to begin are the Women's International Democratic Federation (WIDF) records held in the United States, China,

France, Holland, Germany, Russia, and Sweden—places where WIDF conferences fostered sharing information, analyses, debates among pro-socialist women.

9. Marian Ramelson, *British Woman in New China: Marion Ramelson's Report on the Asian Women's Conference, Peking, 1949* (London: British Committee, WIDF, 1949).

10. Betty Millard, *Women on Guard: How Women of the World Fight for Peace* (New York: New Century Publisher, 1952).

11. Anjali Arondekar, *For the Record: On Sexuality and the Colonial Archive in India* (Durham, NC: Duke University Press, 2010).

12. Francisca de Haan, "Continuing Cold War Paradigms in Western Historiography of Transnational Women's Organizations: The Case of the Women's International Democratic Federation (WIDF)," *Women's History Review* 19, no. 4 (2010): 547–73.

CHAPTER 1

1. Suzy Kim, "The Origins of Cold War Feminism During the Korean War," *Gender & History* 31, no. 2 (July 2019): 460–79; Jacqueline Castledine, *Cold War Progressives: Women's Interracial Organizing for Peace and Freedom* (Champaign: University of Illinois Press, 2012).

2. Marion Ramelson, "Report on Conference of Women of Asia and China," Communist Party of Great Britain, Women's Bureau, Labor History Archives, Manchester, UK. Hereafter, Communist Party of Great Britain, Women's Bureau.

3. Gargi Chakravartty, "Emergence of Mahila Atma Raksha Samiti in the Forties—Calcutta Chapter," in *Calcutta: The Stormy Decades,* ed. Tanika Sarkar and Sekhar Bandyopadhyay (New Delhi: Social Science Press, 2015), 179.

4. *To Women the World Over! Report of the Women's Anti-Fascist Meeting Held in Moscow on September, 7, 1941* (Moscow: Foreign Languages Publishing House, 1941).

5. Soma Marik, "Breaking Through a Double Invisibility: The Communist Women of Bengal, 1939–1948," *Critical Asian Studies* 45, no. 1 (2013): 103. This is Marik's translation of "social" as synonymous to "class."

6. Marik, "Breaking Through a Double Invisibility," 103.

7. Renu Chakravartty, *Communists in Indian Women's Movement, 1940–1950* (New Delhi: People's Publishing House, 1980), 23.

8. Manikuntala Sen, *In Search of Freedom: An Unfinished Journey.* (Kolkata: Stree Press, 2001), 71.

9. Madhusree Mukerjee, *Churchill's Secret War: The British Empire and the Ravaging of India during World War II* (Chennai: Tranquebar Press, 2010), 68.

10. FDIF, *Congress International des Femmes,* International Women's Congress: Minutes of the Congress held in Paris, from November 26 to December 1, 1945 (Paris: FDIF, 1946), Féderation Démocratique Internationale des Femmes (FDIF) Collection, Atria Institute on Gender Equality and Women's History, Amsterdam, Netherlands. Hereafter, FDIF collection.

11. Duong The Hauh, *Congress International des Femmes,* 1945, 175, FDIF collection. Unless otherwise noted, I will keep the transliteration of delegates' names as printed in WIDF documents.

12. Ela Reid came from MARS, Jai Kishore Handoo represented the All India Women's Conference (AIWC), Roshan Barber joined from the India League's London Office, and Vidya Kanuga (Vidya Munsi after her marriage) from the All India Students' Federation. She became an active member of NFIW. MARS joined WIDF during the opening Congress, the only Indian group to do so.

13. Vidya Munsi, *In Retrospect: War-time Memories and Thoughts on Women's Movement* (Kolkata: Manishi Press, 2006), 74.

14. WIDF, *Congress International des Femmes,* 1945, 176, FDIF collection.

15. WIDF, *Congress International des Femmes,* 150, FDIF collection.

16. WIDF, *Congress International des Femmes,* 151, FDIF collection.

17. Adeline Broussan, "'Resistantes' Against the Colonial Order: Women's Grassroots Diplomacy During the French War in Vietnam (1945–1954)," in *The Lives of Cold War Afro-Asianism,* ed. Su Lin Lewis and Carolien Stolte (Leiden: University of Leiden Press, forthcoming).

18. In South Africa alone, the movement of women was gaining coherence and support in the African National Congress and beyond. For archival materials about their activism, see the "History of Women's

Struggle in South Africa" collection of digital resources, South Africa History Online, https://www.sahistory.org.za/collections/16658, accessed December 30, 2021.

19. WIDF, *Congress International des Femmes,* 145, FDIF collection.

20. Vivian Carter Mason, Jai Kishore Handoo, and Jeanne Merens, "Situation of Women in the Colonies and the Issue of Racial Discrimination," *Information Bulletin* 9–10 (October-November 1946): 8.

21. "First Session of the WIDF council, February 21–26, 1947," *Bulletin D'Information,* nos. 14–15 (March-April, 1947): 11, FDIF collection.

22. "First Session of the WIDF council," FDIF collection.

23. "The WIDF Commission in Colonial Countries," *Bulletin D'Information,* no. 21 (October 1947): 3, FDIF collection.

24. The committee included Simone Bertrand (Union of French Women), Pat Miles (WIDF Coordinating Committee), Zelma Brandt (Congress of American Women), and Tamara Morozova (Soviet Women's Anti-Fascist Committee).

25. "The Women of Asia and Africa: Documents," p. 148, FDIF collection.

26. Carolien Stolte, "'The Asiatic Hour': New Perspectives on the Asian Relations Conference, New Delhi, 1947," *The Non-Aligned Movement and the Cold War, Delhi—Bandung—Belgrade,* ed. Natasa Miskovic, Harald Fischer-Tine, and Nada Boskovska (New York: Routledge, 2014), 57–75.

27. Lu Cui, "Coming Back from India," *Bulletin D'Information* 32 (November 1948): 6, FDIF collection. In the *Bulletin,* her name is spelled Tsui, but for this book I use the Pinyin transliteration style for all Chinese names.

28. "The Asian Conference Will Be Held in China," *Bulletin D'Information* 37 (June 1949): 1, Left Federation of Swedish Women.

29. "The Asian Conference Will Be Held in China."

30. CIA, "Women's Groups Prepare for Asian Women's Delegates Conference," October 24-December 2, 1949. Approved for release, September 28, 2011: CIA-RDP80–00809A000600280340–3.

31. Anezka Hodinova-Spurna, "From the People's Democracies," *Information Bulletin* Special Issue (April 1950): 39, Left Federation of Swedish Women.

32. WIDF Commission Report, "The Women of Asia and Africa, Documents," Budapest, December, 1948, FDIF collection.

33. The Resolution was signed by WIDF members including Lu Cui from China, Sarah Abraham from India, Miriam Firouz from Iran, Thai Thi Lien from Vietnam, and Zelma Brandt from the United States, as well as delegates from Holland, Great Britain, Algeria, USSR, Korea, Hungary, France, and Italy.

34. WIDF, *Second Women's International Congress Proceedings, Budapest, Hungary, December, 1948.* Paris: WIDF, 1949, 493. Communism, Socialism and Radical Left Politics Collection, SSC, Box 3, my emphasis. Hereafter, Communism Collection.

35. WIDF, *Second Women's International Congress Proceedings,* 476.

36. WIDF, *Second Women's International Congress Proceedings,* 474.

37. From Lenin's "Speech on the National Question," The Seventh All-Russia Conference, April 29, 1917: "No nation can be free that oppresses other nations."

38. At the founding conference of the USSR's Cominform in August, 1947, Zhdanov outlined a two-camp theory of the world order driven by the United States for the imperialist camp, and congealing around the USSR for the democratic camp. Fascism, colonialism, imperialist expansion, and war marked the former, and the fight for labor, peace, democracy, and national liberation defined the latter. Andrei Zhdanov, "Report on the International Situation to the Cominform," September 22, 1947.

39. Larisa Efimova and Ruth McVey, "Stalin and the New Program for the Communist Party of Indonesia," *Indonesia* 91 (2011): 131–63.

40. WIDF, *Second Women's International Congress Proceedings,* 488.

41. WIDF, *Second Women's International Congress Proceedings,* 475.

42. WIDF, *Second Women's International Congress Proceedings,* 480.

43. WIDF, *Second Women's International Congress Proceedings,* 479.

44. WIDF, *Second Women's International Congress Proceedings,* 476.

45. WIDF, *Second Women's International Congress Proceedings,* 75.

46. WIDF, *Second Women's International Congress Proceedings,* 112.

47. WIDF, *Second Women's International Congress Proceedings,* 183.

48. WIDF, *Second Women's International Congress Proceedings,* 177.

49. WIDF, *Second Women's International Congress Proceedings,* 235–36.

50. WIDF, *Second Women's International Congress Proceedings*, 216.
51. WIDF, *Second Women's International Congress Proceedings*, 210.
52. WIDF, *Second Women's International Congress Proceedings*, 208–9.
53. WIDF, *Second Women's International Congress Proceedings*, 210.
54. WIDF, *Second Women's International Congress Proceedings*, 493.
55. See, for example, the "Report on the Defense of Economic and Political Rights of Women," which invokes working women's conditions in Asia and Africa from a distance: "Our consciences, our feelings of indignation, force us to call the attention of the women of the entire world to the condition of slavery of our sisters in the colonial and dependent countries..." (*Second Women's International Congress*, 288).
56. Cheryl Johnson-Odim and Nina Emma Mba, *For Women and the Nation: Funmilayo Ransome-Duti of Nigeria* (Urbana: University of Illinois Press, 1997), 139.
57. Eslanda Robeson papers, "Writings by—1950 February 15 Trip," Eslanda Goode Robeson Collection.
58. Barbara Ransby, *Eslanda: The Large and Unconventional Life of Mrs. Paul Robeson* (New Haven, CT: Yale University Press, 2013), 200–1.
59. "Writings by—1950 Korea," Eslanda Goode Robeson Collection.
60. "Macarthur sent the American Army into South Korea to fight on Saturday, June 24th. The following Sunday afternoon, the Security Council of the United Nations was called into emergency session and had a hard time taking action because Russia wasn't there, China was not properly represented, and France had no Cabinet at the moment. Yet on the following Monday morning, June 26th, President Truman announced to the world that the United Nations had declared military sanctions against North Korea, and the United States Army had therefore nobly gone to war to carry out the United Nations' orders" ("Writings by—1950 Korea").
61. "Writings by—1950 Korea."
62. "Writings by—1950 Korea."
63. "The Women's International Democratic Federation, Its Aims and Activities, 1945–54," FO 975/74, National Archives, Kew, UK.
64. Taewoo Kim, "Frustrated Peace: Investigatory Activities By the Commission of the Women's International Democratic Federation

(WIDF) in North Korea During the Korean War," *Sungkyun Journal of East Asian Studies* 20, no. 1 (April 2020): 84.

CHAPTER 2

1. Utsa Patnaik and Prabhat Patnaik, "Imperialism in an Era of Globalization," *Monthly Review* 67, no. 3 (July-August, 2015): 68–81.

2. Many of the women changed their last names due to marriage either just before the conference, or afterwards. So, in the comradely and affectionate spirit of the conference-goers, I will use both the delegates' first and last names to describe their contributions.

3. "De Slachtoffers Van Madiun (The Victims of Madiun)," *De Waarheid,* October 30, 1950. *De Waarheid,* or *Truth,* was the newspaper of the Communist Party of the Netherlands.

4. Dutch DocuChannel, "Indonesians in the Dutch Resistance Against the Nazis," Facebook post, February 25, 2021, accessed July 12, 2021, https://www.facebook.com/permalink.php?story_fbid=pfbid025M TZSvkVvMCQRMGyzANitYTUU9DZ7UvQwxTNJyVAzDE7hqFabR 6qNSUpxndcAeJ9l&id=1433706693509457.

5. Eslanda Goode Robeson, China 1950 Diary, Box 17, Eslanda Goode Robeson Collection.

6. Eslanda Goode Robeson, China 1950 Diary.

7. Eslanda Goode Robeson, China 1950 Diary.

8. WIDF, *Second Women's International Congress Proceedings, Budapest, Hungary, December, 1948.* Paris: WIDF, 1949, 503, Communism, Socialism and Radical Left Politics Collection, SSC, Box 3.

9. Dutch DocuChannel, "Indonesians in the Dutch Resistance Against the Nazis." The contingent was named after an Indonesian hero.

10. Harry Poeze, "1940–1945 Isolement en solidariteit," in *In Het Land van de Overheerser: Indonesiers in Nederland 1600–1950* (Leiden: Brill, 1986), 315.

11. Millard Collection, SSC.

12. Millard Collection, SSC.

13. Hendri F. Isnaeni, "Menolak Membantu Agent CIA Pertama di Indonesia" ("Refused to Help Indonesia's First CIA Agent"), February

6, 2021, Historia.id, accessed July 10, 2021, https://historia.id/politik/articles/menolak-membantu-agen-cia-pertama-di-indonesia-vg8dZ.

14. China 1950 Diary, Eslanda Goode Robeson Collection.

15. Millard Collection, SSC.

16. Millard Collection, SSC.

17. Soejono and Ben Anderson, "On Musso's Return," *Indonesia* 29 (April 1980): 78.

18. Ann Swift, *The Road to Madiun: The Indonesian Communist Uprising of 1948* (Ithaca, NY: Monograph Series, Cornell Modern Indonesia project, Cornell University, 1989), 34–36.

19. Swift, *The Road to Madiun*, 34–36.

20. Swift, *The Road to Madiun*, 90.

21. Millard Collection, SSC.

22. At the time, Shenyang was called Mukden.

23. Millard Collection, SSC.

24. Suzy Kim describes another train contingent to the conference, this one leaving from Pyongyang, North Korea, with over forty delegates and fifty-eight performers on board. See *Among Women, Across Worlds: North Korea in the Global Cold War* (Ithaca, New York: Cornell University Press, 2022), 67.

25. The women who arrived in Beijing after the conference ended included the delegates from the Vietnamese Women's Union. Van Thi Lien was the president of the cultural section of the Union of Vietnamese Women; Nguyen Khoa Dien Hong was the vice president of the Union of Vietnamese Women; Dao Van Chau was the president of the Union of Women of Vietnam, in Paris. The delegation also included Phan Thi An and Hyunh Boi Hoan.

26. Union of Viet-Name (sic) Women in France, "Women of Viet-Nam in the Struggle for the Safeguard of Independence" (Paris: Union of Vietnam Women in France, 1948).

27. Pham Ngoc Thuan, *2nd Women's International Congress of WIDF, Budapest, Hungary, 1948*, 493, Communism Collection.

28. Betty Millard, "Prague to Shanghai—A New World Voyage," *Daily Worker*, Monday, April 17, 1950, 5, Millard Collection, SSC.

29. Eslanda Goode Robeson, China 1950 Diary.

30. Mire Koikari, *Pedagogy of Democracy: Feminism and the Cold War in the US Occupation of Japan* (Philadelphia: Temple University Press, 2008), 151–57.

31. Koikari, *Pedagogy of Democracy*, 156.

32. Ho Thi Minh, "In Waging Armed Struggle for National Independence We Will Win Peace," *Information Bulletin* Special Issue (April 1950): 15, Left Federation of Swedish Women.

CHAPTER 3

1. Millard Collection, SSC.

2. Wang Zheng, *Finding Women in the State: A Socialist Feminist Revolution in the People's Republic of China, 1949–1964* (Berkeley: University of California Press, 2017): 156, 159–65.

3. Millard Collection, SSC.

4. WIDF conference notes, December 21, 1949, Left Federation of Swedish Women.

5. They included women from West Asia, such as Salma Boummi and Amine Aref Hasan (Syrian Arab Women's Union), Victoria Helou (League for the Defense of the Right of Lebanese Women), Ruth Lubitsh and Ilanit Feyga (Association of Arab Women of Israel or Nahda) and Mahine Faroqi (from the banned Organization of Iranian Women). Delegates came from the six Asiatic Republics of the USSR, such as Naila Basanova from Kazakistan, Kulipa Toklomanbetova from Kirghizia, Acia Atapanova from Turkmenia, and Mikrinis Ubaydulasva from Uzbekistan, as well as delegates from Azerbaijan and Tadjikistan. Among the thirty-three fraternal (non-Asian) delegates, several came from the USSR and from one Eastern European socialist country—Czechoslovakia. Others came from Algeria, Cuba, England, France, Holland, Ivory Coast, Madagascar, and the United States. The delegate from Cuba was Edith García Buchaca, a member of the communist Partido Socialista Popular. MacArthur's occupation of Japan denied visas to the delegation of the Japanese Democratic Women's Council, so one Japanese woman who lived permanently in China stood in for them.

6. Ho Thi Minh, "In Waging Armed Struggle for National Independence We Will Win Peace," *Information Bulletin* Special Issue (April 1950): 15, Left Federation of Swedish Women.

7. "Women in the Democratic Republic of Viet Nam," *Information Bulletin* Special Issue (April 1950): 16, Left Federation of Swedish Women.

8. "To Our Sisters!," *Information Bulletin* Special Issue (April 1950): 9, Left Federation of Swedish Women.

9. "To Our Sisters!," 9.

10. Ramelson notes, Communist Party of Great Britain, Women's Bureau.

11. Andrea Andreen, in WIDF, *Second Women's International Congress Proceedings, Budapest, Hungary, December, 1948.* Paris: WIDF, 1949, 149, Communism, Socialism and Radical Left Politics Collection, SSC, Box 3.

12. WIDF, *Second Women's International Congress Proceedings*, 12.

13. Jacqueline Castledine, *Cold War Progressives: Women's Interracial Organizing for Peace and* Freedom (Urbana-Champaign: University of Illinois Press, 2012); Erik McDuffie, *Sojourning for Freedom: Black Women, American Communism, and the Making of Black Left Feminism* (Durham, NC: Duke University Press, 2011): 160–93; Kate Weigand, *Red Feminism: American Communism and the Making of Women's Liberation* (Baltimore: Johns Hopkins Press, 2001), 46–64.

14. "March 8 1950," *Information Bulletin* 42 (January-February 1950): 1, Left Federation of Swedish Women.

15. Left Federation of Swedish Women.

16. Lillah Suripno, "Soekarno and Hatta—Puppets of the Dutch and American Imperialists," *Information Bulletin* Special Issue (April 1950): 26, Left Federation of Swedish Women.

17. Ramelson notes, Communist Party of Great Britain, Women's Bureau.

18. "News: From the Conference of the Women of Asia: International Solidarity December 28, 1949," Left Federation of Swedish Women.

19. Jeannette Vermeersch, *The Trial of French Colonialism* (Rangoon, Burma: Vietnam News Service, 1950).

20. Dieter Heinzig, *The Soviet Union and Communist China, 1945–1950* (Armonk, NY: M.E. Sharpe, 2004).

21. Suzy Kim, "The Origins of Cold War Feminism during the Korean War," *Gender and History* 31, no. 2 (July 2019): 461.

22. "News: From the Conference of the Women of Asia: International Solidarity, December 28, 1949," 3, Left Federation of Swedish Women.

23. Appeal issued by the Conference, "To Our Sisters, the Women of the Countries of Asia," *Information Bulletin* Special Issue (April 1950): 7, Left Federation of Swedish Women Papers.

24. Chen Xiu Zhu oral history in Agnes Khoo, *Life as the River Flows: Women in the Malayan Anti-Colonial Struggle* (Monmouth, Wales: Merlin Press, 2007), 67.

25. WIDF, *Second Women's International Congress Proceedings,* 487.

26. Lu Cui and Deng Yingchao, 2nd Session of the Asian Women's Conference, December 11, 1949, Ramelson notes, Communist Party of Great Britain, Women's Bureau.

27. Wang, *Finding Women in the State,* 13–14.

28. Wang, *Finding Women in the State,* 13–14.

29. Ruth McVey, "The Calcutta Conference and the Southeast Asian Uprisings," Interim Reports Series, Department of Far Eastern Studies, Cornell University, 1958, p. 1. For confirmation of this earlier assessment that includes recently released documents from Russian archives, see Larisa Efimova, "Did the Soviet Union Instruct Southeast Asian Communists to Revolt? New Russian Evidence on the Calcutta Youth Conference of February 1948," *Journal of Southeast Asian Studies* 40, no. 3 (October, 2009): 449–69.

30. Deng Yingchao, "The Struggle of the Women in the Countries of Asia for National Independence, Democracy and Peace," *Information Bulletin* Special Issue (April, 1950): 3, Left Federation of Swedish Women.

31. Pak Chong-ae, "With the total support of the peoples... We are fighting to unify our entire land under the People's Republic of Korea," *Information Bulletin* Special Issue (April 1950): 37,47, Left Federation of Swedish Women.

32. Suzy Kim, *Everyday Life in the North Korean Revolution, 1945–1950* (Ithaca, NY: Cornell University Press, 2013).

33. Kim, *Everyday Life in the North Korean Revolution,* 243.

34. Ramelson notes, Women's Bureau, Communist Party of Great Britain Papers.

35. Gisele Rabesahala, "In Madagascar, Drenched in Blood, the People Refuse to be Accomplices of the Imperialists," *Information Bulletin* Special Issue (April 1950): 35, 47, Left Federation of Swedish Women.

36. Baya Allaouchiche, "We, too, want to win our place in life ... 'Peace is the straightest Road to National Liberation for the Algerian People,'" *Information Bulletin* Special Issue (April 1950): 38, Left Federation of Swedish Women.

37. Ramelson notes, Communist Party of Great Britain, Women's Bureau.

38. Ramelson notes, Communist Party of Great Britain, Women's Bureau.

39. Ramelson notes, Communist Party of Great Britain, Women's Bureau.

40. Rabesahala, "In Madagascar, Drenched in Blood."

CHAPTER 4

1. Gita Bandyopadhyay's name was most commonly spelled Bannerji in the WIDF's publications. I use her own spelling of her name.

2. Ratnabali Chatterjee, "Gita Bandyopadhyay: Memories and Impressions," personal correspondence, 2021.

3. Gita Bandyopadhyay, *Ek Dub Dui Dub* (Kolkata: Kabi Pokkho, 1998), translated to English from Bengali by Sarbajaya Bhattacharya, 2021.

4. Manikuntala Sen, *In Search of Freedom: An Unfinished Journey* (Calcutta: Stree, 2001), 120–1; Gargi Chakravartty, "Emergence of Mahila Atma Raksha Samiti in the Forties—Calcutta Chapter," in *Calcutta: The Stormy Decades*, ed. Tanika Sarkar and Sekhar Bandyopadhyay (New Delhi: Social Science Press, 2015), 177–203.

5. Bandyopadhyay, *Ek Dub Dui Dub*.

6. Soma Marik, "Breaking Through a Double Invisibility: The Communist Women of Bengal, 1939–1948," *Critical Asian Studies* 45, no. 1 (2013): 79–118.

7. Bandyopadhyay, *Ek Dub Dui Dub*. Section 144 of the Criminal Procedure Code was used to ban political activity in India.

8. E.M.S. Namboodiripad, *A History of Indian Freedom Struggle* (Trivandrum, Kerala: Social Scientist Press, 1986). These speeches and writings by a leading communist theorist and activist throughout the latter half of the twentieth century were first published in Malayalam in 1977, and translated into English for publication in 1986. The articles were originally published serially from the 1950s to the 1970s in *New Age Monthly*. Also see Namboodiripad's book *Economics and Politics of India's Socialist Pattern* for analysis directly after Indian independence in 1947.

9. National Union of Students, "Co-ordinating Council for Colonial Students' Affairs," letter to solicit support for a demonstration for "Indonesian freedom and (to) show their solidarity with the Indonesian youth struggling against colonialism," written by Mina Sen, Secretary, January 11, 1949. The National Archives, London, UK, Accession Number CP 537/4381.

10. Ruth McVey, "The Calcutta Conference and the Southeast Asian Uprisings," Interim Report Series, Modern Indonesia Project, Ithaca, NY: Cornell University, 1958; Tuong Vu, "'It's Time for the Indochinese Revolution to Show Its True Colors': The Radical Turn of Vietnamese Politics in 1948," *Journal of Southeast Asian Studies* 40, no. 3 (October 2009): 519–42; Larisa Efimova, "Did the Soviet Union Instruct Southeast Asian Communists to Revolt? New Russian Evidence on the Calcutta Youth Conference of February 1948," *Journal of Southeast Asian Studies* 40, no. 3 (October 2009): 449–69.

11. Elisabeth Armstrong, "Before Bandung: The Anti-Imperialist Women's Movement in Asia and the Women's International Democratic Federation," *Signs: Journal of Women in Culture and Society* 41, no. 2 (Winter 2016): 305–32.

12. Women's International Democratic Federation South East Asian Women's Conference, KPM/SB/4671/08, Special Branch files, Calcutta Police, Kolkata Police Museum Archive, Kolkata, India. Thanks to Suchetana Chattopadhyay for sharing the Women's International Democratic Federation files with me.

13. Adrienne Cooper, *Sharecropping and Sharecroppers' Struggles in Bengal, 1930-1950* (Kolkata: KP Bagchi, 1988); Peter Custers, *Women in the*

Tebhaga Uprising: Rural Poor Women and Revolutionary Leadership, 1946-47 (Kolkata: Naya Prokash, 1987); Yasmine Khan, "Sex in an Imperial War Zone: Transnational Encounters in Second World War India," *History Workshop Journal* 73, no. 1 (2012): 240–58.

14. Sonali Satpathi, "Mobilizing Women: The Experience of the Left in West Bengal, 1947-1964," PhD diss., University of Calcutta, 2013.

15. Renu Chakkravartty, *Communists in Indian Women's Movement* (New Delhi: People's Publishing House, 1980).

16. Adeline Broussan, "Resistantes Against the Colonial Order: Women's Grassroots Diplomacy During the French War in Vietnam (1945–1954)," in *The Lives of Cold War Afro-Asianism*, ed. Su Lin Lewis and Carolien Stolte (Leiden: University of Leiden Press, 2022).

17. Gita Bandyopadhyay, letter to Betty Millard, July 1, 1954, Millard Collection, SSC.

18. Gita Bandyopadhyay, letter to Betty Millard, July 1, 1954, Millard Collection, SSC.

19. Bruce Cumings, *The Origins of the Korean War* (Princeton, NJ: Princeton University Press, 1990), 2:568–621.

20. Suzy Kim, *Everyday Life in the North Korean Revolution, 1945–1950* (Ithaca, NY: Cornell University Press, 2013).

21. Suzy Kim, "The Origins of Cold War Feminism During the Korean War," *Gender and History* 31, no. 2 (July 2019): 461.

22. Michelle Chase, "'Hands Off Korea!': Women's Internationalist Solidarity and Peace Activism in Early Cold War Cuba," *Journal of Women's History* 32, no. 3 (Fall 2020): 64–88.

23. "The Situation of Women in Colonies, Discussions on Racial Discrimination," *Bulletin d'Information.* 9–10 (Octobre-Novembre, 1946): 7. FDIF Collection. Vivian Carter Mason, the US representative to WIDF from the National Council of Negro Women (NCNW); Jeanne Merens, a communist and founder of the Algerian Women's Union; and Jai Kishore Handoo, a member of the Women's Commnittee of India League in London, developed early materials for the WIDF executive committee meeting focused on anti-colonialism and anti-racism.

24. R. Palme Dutt, *Fascism and Social Revolution* (San Francisco: Proletarian Publisher, 1934), 102.

25. WIDF Preparatory Committee for the Conference of the Women of Asia, *The Women of Asia and Africa* (Budapest: WIDF, 1948).

26. WIDF Preparatory Committee for the Conference of the Women of Asia, *The Women of Asia and Africa.*

27. Gita Bandyopadhyay, letter to Betty Millard, March 5, 1951, Millard Collection, SSC.

28. Gita Bandyopadhyay, letter to Betty Millard, March 5, 1951, Millard Collection, SSC.

29. Gita Bandyopadhyay, letter to Betty Millard, September 6, 1950, Millard Collection, SSC.

30. Betty Millard, letter to her mother (copy), April 2, 1950, Millard Collection, SSC.

31. "We Accuse! Report of the Commission of the Women's International Democratic Federation in Korea, May 16 to 27, 1951 (Berlin: WIDF, 1951). See also "The Children of Korea: Call to the Women of the World," another pamphlet published by WIDF in 1951 with an appeal for humanitarian support for the Korean people, particularly mothers and children. The WIDF official report, delivered to the United Nations, was also published in 1951. "Report of the Women's International Commission for the Investigation of Atrocities Committed by the USA and Syngmann Rhee Troops in Korea," The Delegation, Korea II, Box 60, Folder 2, Reference Center for Marxist Studies Pamphlet Collection, Tamiment Library and Robert Wagner Labor Archives.

32. Taewoo Kim, "Frustrated Peace: Investigatory Activities by the Commission of the Women's International Democratic Federation (WIDF) in North Korea During the Korean War," *Singkyun Journal of East Asian Studies.* 20, no. 1 (April 2020): 83–112.

33. T. Kim, "Frustrated Peace," 84.

34. Chase, "Hands Off Korea!," 81.

35. Young-Sun Hong, *Cold War Germany, the Third World, and the Global Humanitarian Regime* (New York: Cambridge University Press, 2015), 54.

36. Chase, "Hands Off Korea!," 71.

37. Many of the members of CAW reconfigured as part of American Women for Peace to maintain their activism during the McCarthy period. Their newsletter, *The Peacemaker,* dedicated one issue to the WIDF contingent that toured Korea and reported on the carnage. An

article titled "Negro G.I.s Question Korea" demanded an end to racist wars in Asia and Africa: "We think that we Negroes, who are asked to fight wars in Asia and Europe but who are not free at home should have our say before it is too late. If enough of us can get together, we believe we will get our peace and freedom too." The editorial stated: "We who are aware of the effects of these things, and who love our country look with horror on the death and misery which has resulted from our war policy. We cry out." See "Editorial: U.S. Bankrupt Policy," *The Peacemaker* 2, no. 8 (September 1951), Millard Collection, SSC

38. Claudia Jones, "International Women's Day and the Struggle for Peace," *Political Affairs* 29, no. 3 (1950): 32–45.

39. Claudia Jones, "Speech to the Court, February, 1953," *Thirteen Communists Speak in Court* (New York: New Century Publications, 1953): 121.

40. Gargi Chakravartty, "Emergence of Mahila Atma Raksha Samiti in the Forties—Calcutta Chapter," in *The Stormy Decades: Calcutta,* ed. Tanika Sarkar and Sekhar Bandyopadhyay (New Delhi: Social Science Press, 2015), 202.

41. Statistics are from the CPI newspaper *Swadhinata Patrika,* cited in Satpathi, "Mobilizing Women," 202.

42. Gita Bandyopadhyay, letter to Betty Millard, October 24, 1951, Betty Millard Collection, SSC.

43. Gita Bandyopadhyay, letter to Betty Millard, June 6, 1953, Betty Millard Collection, SSC.

44. Su Lin Lewis, "Asian Socialism and the Forgotten Architects of Post-Colonial Freedom, 1952–1956," and Rachel Leow, "A Missing Peace: The Asia-Pacific Peace Conference in Beijing, 1952 and the Emotional Making of Third World Internationalism," in *The Lives of Cold War Afro-Asianism,* ed. Su Lin Lewis and Carolien Stolte (Leiden: University of Leiden Press, 2022).

CONCLUSION

1. Celestine Ouezzin Coulibaly, "To Put an End to the Society of Masters and Serfs," *Information Bulletin* Special Issue (April 1950): 48, Left Federation of Swedish Women.

2. Destiny Wiley-Yancy, "Afro-Asian Peoples' Solidarity Organization (AAPSO) Presidium Committee Nairobi Preparations," *Meridians* 20, no. 1 (April 2021): 174–82.

3. For these insights and primary research, I credit Smith students Becca Alonso, Lucìa Gonzàlez, Ramona Flores, Destiny Wiley-Yancy, and Lily Sendroff.

4. Nighat Said Khan, "Up Against the State: The Women's Movement in Pakistan and its Implications for the Global Women's Movement," in *Politics, Activism and Vision: Local and Global Challenges,* ed. Luciana Ricciutelli, Angela Miles, and Margaret H. McFadden (London: Zed Books, 2004), 86.

SOURCES AND FURTHER READING

ARCHIVES

Amherst, Massachusetts, United States
  Special Collections and University Archives, University of Massachusetts, Amherst
    James Aronson Collection of W. E. B. DuBois
    James H. and Sibylle Fraser Collection

Amsterdam, Netherlands
  Atria Institute on Gender Equality and Women's History
    Women's International Democratic Federation
    International Archives for the Women's Movement
  International Institute of Social History Archives
    Women's International Democratic Federation

Beirut, Lebanon
  American University in Beirut Archives
    Genevieve Maxwell Papers
    Political posters collection
    Linda Sadaqa Papers
    Mary Winfred Papers
    Women's Auxiliary Papers
    Women's League Papers

Constantine Zurayk Papers
Huddinge, Sweden
   Swedish Labor Movement Archives
      The Left Federation of Swedish Women Papers
Kolkata, India
   Kolkata Police Museum Archive, Special Branch files, Calcutta Police
      Women's International Democratic Federation Papers
London, United Kingdom
   The British Library
      India Office Archives
   The National Archives
      National Assembly of Women
      Tamara Rust Papers, India Office Archives
   University of London, SOAS, Special Collections
      Liberation Archive
      Movement for Colonial Freedom papers
Manchester, UK
   People's History Museum, Labor History Archive (PHM)
      Communist Party of Great Britain Collection
New Delhi, India
   Nehru Memorial Museum and Library Archives
      Bengal Review Committee Report, 1943–45
      All India Women's Commission
      Hansa Mehta Papers
      Kamala Chattopadhyay Papers
      Oral History Project
      Peasant Movement Papers
      Renuka Ray Papers
   P.C. Joshi Archives on Contemporary History, Jawaharlal Nehru University
      Books, articles and pamphlets on China
      Books, articles and pamphlets on Indian Communism
      Journal and periodical collection
      Kisan: Pamphlets and Reports of the All India Kisan Sabha
      League Against Imperialism Papers

World Communism Papers
Peace and Solidarity Papers
New York City, United States
   Tamiment Library & Wagner Labor Archives
      Ephemera Collection on the Communist Party of the United States of America
      James E. Jackson and Esther Cooper Jackson Photographs
      Reference Center for Marxist Studies Pamphlet Collection
      Anna Louise Strong Papers
Northampton, Massachusetts, United States
   Sophia Smith Collection of Women's History, Smith College
      Committee of Correspondence Records
      Communism, Socialism and Radical Left Politics Collection
      Countries Collection
      Dorothy Kenyon Papers
      Betty Millard Papers
      Pan Pacific and Southeast Asia Women's Association of the U.S.A. Records
      Ruth Francis Woodsmall Papers
      Women's International Democratic Federation Records
Washington, DC, United States
   Moorland-Springarn Research Center, Howard University
      Eslanda Goode Robeson Collection
      Paul Robeson and Eslanda Robeson Collection

SOURCES AND FURTHER READING

Listed below, chapter by chapter, are those sources that were most directly relevant to each section. With very few exceptions, each entry will appear only once, under the chapter where the subject matter is first referred to. At the beginning, under "Introduction," are key sources that were of use throughout the book and provide the necessary context for the global complexities of women's organizations with an affiliation to the Women's International Democratic Federation (WIDF).

Introduction

Barthelemy, Pascale. "Macoucou in Beijing. The International Arena: A Political Resource for African Women in the 1940s and 1950s. *The Social Movement* 255 (April-June 2016): 17–33.

Blain, Keisha, and Tiffany Gill. *To Turn the Whole World Over: Black Women and Internationalism.* Urbana: University of Illinois Press, 2019.

Bonfiglioli, Chiara. "Revolutionary Networks: Women's Political and Social Activism in Cold War Italy and Yugoslavia (1945-1957)." PhD diss., Utrecht University, 2012.

Broussan, Adeline. "'Resistantes' Against the Colonial Order: Women's Grassroots Diplomacy During the French War in Vietnam (1945–1954)." In *The Lives of Cold War Afro-Asianism,* edited by Su Lin Lewis and Carolien Stolte. Leiden: University of Leiden Press, 2022.

Castledine, Jacqueline. "'In a Solid Bond of Unity': Anti-Colonial Feminism in the Cold War Era." *Journal of Women's History* 20, no. 4 (2008): 57–81.

Chakravartty, Gargi, and Supriya Chotani. *Charting a New Path: Early Years of National Federation of Indian Women.* New Delhi: People's Publishing House, 2014.

Chakkravartty, Renu. *Communists in Indian Women's Movement.* New Delhi: People's Publishing House, 1980.

Chase, Michelle. "'Hands Off Korea!': Women's Internationalist Solidarity and Peace Activism in Early Cold War Cuba." *Journal of Women's History* 32, no. 3 (2020): 64–88.

Dang, Vimla. *Fragments of an Autobiography.* Delhi: Asha Jyoti, 2007.

Davies, Carole Boyce, ed. *Claudia Jones: Beyond Containment.* Banbury: Ayebia Clarke Press, 2011.

———. *Left of Karl Marx: The Political Life of Black Communist Claudia Jones.* Durham, NC: Duke University Press, 2008.

de Haan, Francisca. "Continuing Cold War Paradigms in Western Historiography of Transnational Women's Organizations: The Case of the Women's International Democratic Federation (WIDF)." *Women's History Review* 19, no. 4 (2010): 547–73.

---. "Eugenie Cotton, Pak Chong-Ae, and Claudia Jones: Rethinking Transnational Feminism and International Politics." *Journal of Women's History* 25, no. 4 (Winter 2013): 174–89.

---. "The Vietnam Activities of the Women's International Democratic Federation (WIDF)." In *Protest in the Vietnam War Era*, edited by Alexander Sedlmaier, 51–82. New York: Palgrave.

Donert, Celia. "From Communist Internationalism to Human Rights: Gender, Violence and International Law in the Women's International Democratic Federation Mission to North Korea, 1951." *Contemporary European History* 25, no. 2 (2016): 313–33.

Foll-Luciani, Pierre-Jean. "'I Wish I Had Been a Bomb to Explode': Algerian Communist Militants Between Sexual Assignments and Subversions of Gender Roles (1944–1962)." *The Social Movement* 225 (April-June 2016): 35–55.

Funk, Nanette. "A Very Tangled Knot: Official State Socialist Women's Organizations, Women's Agency and Feminism in Eastern European State Socialist Feminism." *European Journal of Women's Studies* 21, no. 4 (2014): 344–60.

Ghodsee, Kristen. *Second World, Second Sex: Socialist Women's Activism and Global Solidarity During the Cold War*. Durham, NC: Duke University Press, 2019.

---. "Research Note: The Historiographical Challenges of Exploring Second World-Third World Alliances in the International Women's Movement." *Global Social Policy* 14, no. 2 (2014): 244–64.

---. "Untangling the Knot: A Response to Nanette Funk." *European Journal of Women's Studies* 22, no. 2 (2015): 248–52.

Gilyard, Keith. *Louise Thompson Patterson: A Life of Struggle for Justice*. Durham, NC: Duke University Press, 2017.

Gore, Dayo. *Radicalism at the Crossroads: African American Women Activists in the Cold War*. New York: New York University Press, 2011.

Gore, Dayo, Jeanne Theoharis, and Komozi Woodard, ed. *Want to Start a Revolution? Radical Women in the Black Freedom Movement*. New York: New York University Press, 2009.

Gradskova, Yulia. *The Women's International Democratic Federation, the Global South, and the Cold War: Defending the Rights of Women of the 'Whole World'?* New York: Routledge, 2021.

Higashida, Cheryl. *Black Internationalist Feminism: Women Writers of the Black Left, 1945-1995.* Urbana-Champaign: University of Illinois Press, 2013.

Jayawardena, Kumari. *Feminism and Nationalism in the Third World.* London: Zed Press, 1986.

Johnson-Odim, Cheryl, and Nina Emma Mba. *For Women and the Nation: Funmilayo Ransome-Kuti of Nigeria.* Urbana: University of Illinois Press, 1997.

Kim, Suzy. *Among Women Across Worlds: North Korea in the Global Cold War.* Ithaca, NY: Cornell University Press, 2022.

———. "Revolutionary Mothers: Women in the North Korean Revolution, 1945–1950." *Comparative Studies in Society and History* 52, no. 4(October 2010): 742–67.

———. "The Origins of Cold War Feminism During the Korean War." *Gender & History,* 31, no. 2 (July 2019): 460–79.

Kim, Taewoo. "Frustrated Peace: Investigatory Activities By the Commission of the Women's International Democratic Federation (WIDF) in North Korea During the Korean War. *Sungkyun Journal of East Asian Studies.* 20, no.1 (April 2020): 83–112.

McDuffie, Erik. *Sojourning for Freedom: Black Women, American Communism, and the Making of Black Left Feminism.* Durham, NC: Duke University Press, 2011.

McGregor, Katharine. "The Cold War, Indonesian Women and the Global Anti-Imperialist Movement, 1946-65." In *De-Centering Cold War History: Local and Global Change,* edited by Jadwiga Pieper and Fabio Lanza, 31–51. New York: Routledge, 2013.

———. "Indonesian Women, the Women's International Democratic Federation (WIDF) and the Struggle for 'Women's Rights,' 1946-1965." *Indonesia and the Malay World.* 40, no. 117 (2012): 193–208.

———. "Opposing Colonialism: the Women's International Democratic Women's Federation and Decolonization Struggles in Vietnam and Algeria 1945-1965." *Women's History Review* 25, no. 6 (2016): 925–44.

Mooney, Jadwiga Pieper. "Fighting Fascism and Forging New Political Activism: The Women's International Democratic Federation (WIDF) in the Cold War." In *De-Centering Cold War History: Local and Global Change,* edited by Jadwiga Pieper Mooney and Fabio Lanza, 52–72. New York: Routledge, 2013.

Munsi, Vidya. *In Retrospect: War-time Memories and Thoughts on Women's Movement.* Kolkata: Manishi, 2006.

Ransby, Barbara. *Eslanda: The Large and Unconventional Life of Mrs. Paul Robeson.* New Haven, CT: Yale University Press, 2013.

Satpathi, Sonali. "Mobilizing Women: The Experience of the Left in West Bengal, 1947–61," PhD. diss., Calcutta University, 2013.

Sen, Manikuntala. *In Search of Freedom: An Unfinished Journey.* New Delhi: Stree, 2001.

Thompson, Elizabeth. *Colonial Citizens: Republican Rights, Paternal Privilege, and Gender in French Syria and Lebanon.* New York: Columbia University Press, 2000.

Umoren, Imaobong. *Race Women Internationalists: Activist-Intellectuals and Global Freedom Struggles.* Oakland: University of California Press, 2018.

"Vietnamese Women." *Vietnamese Studies, vol. 10.* Hanoi, Democratic Republic of Vietnam, 1966.

Vince, Natalya. *Our Fighting Sisters: Nation, Memory and Gender in Algeria, 1954–2012.* Manchester: Manchester University Press, 2015.

Wang, Zheng. *Finding Women in the State: A Socialist Feminist Revolution in the People's Republic of China, 1949–1964.* Berkeley: University of California Press, 2017.

Washington, Mary Helen. *The Other Blacklist: The African American Literary and Cultural Left of the 1950s.* New York: Columbia University Press, 2014.

Weber, Charlotte. "Making Common Cause?: Western and Middle Eastern Feminists in the International Women's Movement, 1911–1948." PhD diss., Ohio State University, 2003.

Weigand, Kate. *Red Feminism: American Communism and the Making of Women's Liberation.* Baltimore: Johns Hopkins Press, 2000.

Wieringa, Saskia. *Sexual Politics in Indonesia.* New York: Palgrave Macmillan, 2002.

Wu, Judy Tzu-Chun. *Radicals on the Road: Internationalism, Orientalism, and Feminism During the Vietnam Era.* Ithaca, NY: Cornell University Press, 2013.

Yusta, Mercedes. "The Strained Courtship Between Antifascism and Feminism: From the Women's World Committee (1934) to the Women's International Democratic Federation (1945)." In *Rethinking Fascism: History, Memory and Politics, 1922 to the Present*, edited by Hugo Garcia, Mercedes Yusta, Xavier Tabet and Cristina Climaco, 167–84. New York: Berghahn Books, 2016.

Chapter 1

Austin, Gwen Marie. "Embattled But Writing Back: Eslanda Goode Robeson's Contribution to American and International Politics Through Her Writings." 2009. http://cedu.niu.edu/cahe/news/newsDocuments/AALA08_Web/AALA08_Papers/Austin.pdf. Accessed on July 10, 2021.

Boum, Aomar, and Sarah Stein. *The Holocaust and North Africa*. Stanford, CA: Stanford University Press, 2019.

Dimitrov, George. *Against Fascism and War*. New York: International Publishers, 1986.

Dutt, R. Palme. *Fascism and Social Revolution: A Study of the Economics and Politics of the Extreme Stages of Capitalism in Decay*. San Francisco, CA: Proletarian Publishers, 1935.

Efimova, Larisa, and Ruth McVey. "Stalin and the New Program for the Communist Party of Indonesia." *Indonesia* 91 (2011): 131–63.

Fleischmann, Ellen. "The Emergence of the Palestinian Women's Movement, 1929–39." *Journal of Palestine Studies* 30, no. 3 (Spring 2000): 16–32.

French, John, and Mary Lynn Pederson. "Women and Working-Class Mobilization in Postwar Sao Paulo, 1945–1948." *Latin American Research Review* 24, no. 3 (1989): 99–125.

Gaiduk, Ilya V. 2009. "Soviet Cold War Strategy and Prospects of Revolution in Asia." In *Connecting Histories: Decolonization and the Cold War in Southeast Asia, 1945–1962*, edited by Christopher Goscha and Christian Ostermann, 123–36. Stanford, CA: Stanford University Press, 2009.

Hudson, Michael. *Super Imperialism: The Economic Strategy of American Empire*. New York: Holt, Rinehart and Winston, 1972.

Kosambi, D.D. *Exasperating Essays: Exercises in the Dialectical Method.* New Delhi: People's Publishing House, 1957.

Lee, Christopher, ed. *Making a World After Empire: The Bendung Moment and its Political Aftermath.* Athens: Ohio University Press, 2010.

Lenin, V.I. "Speech on the National Question." The Seventh All-Russia Conference, April 29, 1917.

McVey, Ruth. "The Calcutta Conference and the Southeast Asian Uprisings." Interim Reports Series, Department of Far Eastern Studies, Cornell University, 1958.

Munro, John. "Imperial Anticommunism and the African American Freedom Movement in the Early Cold War." *History Workshop Journal* 79 (Spring 2015): 52–75.

Namboodiripad, E.M.S. *A History of Indian Freedom Struggle.* Trivandrum, India: Social Scientist Press, 1986.

———. "The Left in India's Freedom Movement and in Free India." *Social Scientist* 14, nos. 8–9 (August-September, 1986): 3–17.

Perlo, Victor. *American Imperialism.* New York: International Publishers, 1951.

Petersson, Frederick. "Hub of the Anti-Imperialist Movement: The League Against Imperialism and Berlin, 1927–1933." *Interventions* 16, no. 1 (2014): 49–71.

Pomeroy, William. *American Neo-Colonialism: Its Emergence in the Philippines and Asia.* New York: International Publishers, 1970.

———, ed. *Guerilla Warfare and Marxism: A Collection of Writings from Karl Marx to the Present on Armed Struggles for Liberation and for Socialism.* New York: International Publishers, 1968.

Rao, M.B., ed. *Documents of the History of the History of the Communist Party of India, Vol. VII, 1948–1950.* New Delhi: People's Publishing House, 1976.

Selsam, Howard, David Goldway and Harry Martel, eds. *Dynamics of Social Change: A Reader in Marxist Social Science from the Writings of Marx, Engels and Lenin.* New York: International Publishers, 1970.

Sinha, Mrinalini. *Specters of Mother India: The Global Restructuring of an Empire.* Durham, NC: Duke University Press, 2006.

Stolte, Carolien. "'The Asiatic hour': New Perspectives on the Asian Relations Conference, New Delhi, 1947." In *The Non-Aligned*

Movement and the Cold War, Delhi—Bandung—Belgrade, edited by Natasa Miskovic, Harald Fischer-Tine, and Nada Boskovska, 57–75. New York: Routledge, 2014.

Togliatti, Palmiro. *Lectures on Fascism, Revised Edition.* New York: International Publishers, 1976, 2017.

Vermeersch, Jeannette. 1950. *The Trial of French Colonialism.* Rangoon, Burma: Vietnam News Service.

Zhdanov, Andrei. "Report on the International Situation to the Cominform." September 22, 1947.

Chapter 2

Koikari, Mire. *Pedagogy of Democracy: Feminism and the Cold War in the US Occupation of Japan.* Philadelphia: Temple University Press, 2008.

Patnaik, Utsa, and Prabhat Patnaik. "Imperialism in an Era of Globalization." *Monthly Review* 67, no. 3 (July-August, 2015): 68–81.

Poeze, Harry. *In Het Land van de Overheerser: Indonesiers in Nederland 1600–1950.* Leiden: Brill, 1986.

Swift, Ann. *The Road to Madiun: The Indonesian Communist Uprising of 1948.* Ithaca, NY: Monograph Series, Cornell Modern Indonesia project, Cornell University, 1989.

Chapter 3

Dieter, Heinzig. *The Soviet Union and Communist China, 1945–1950.* Armonk, NY: M.E. Sharpe, 2004.

Efimova, Larisa. "Did the Soviet Union Instruct Southeast Asian Communists to Revolt? New Russian Evidence on the Calcutta Youth Conference of February 1948." *Journal of Southeast Asian Studies* 40, no. 3 (October, 2009): 449–69.

Kim, Suzy. *Everyday Life in the North Korean Revolution, 1945–1950.* Ithaca, NY: Cornell University Press, 2013.

Khoo, Agnes. *Life as the River Flows: Women in the Malayan Anti-Colonial Struggle.* Monmouth, Wales: Merlin Press, 2007.

McVey, Ruth. "The Calcutta Conference and the Southeast Asian Uprisings." Interim Reports Series, Department of Far Eastern Studies, Cornell University, 1958.

Munro, John. *The Anticolonial Front: The African American Freedom Struggle and Global Decolonisation, 1945-1960*. Cambridge: Cambridge University Press, 2017.

Prashad, Vijay. *The Darker Nations: A People's History of the Third World*. New York: The New Press, 2007.

———. *The Poorer Nations: A Possible History of the Global South*. New York: Verso, 2012.

Vermeersch, Jeannette. *The Trial of French Colonialism*. Rangoon, Burma: Vietnam News Service, 1950.

Westad, Odd Arne. *The Global Cold War*. Cambridge: Cambridge University Press, 2007.

Chapter 4

"Among Kisan Women." *People's War* 3, no. 46 (May 13, 1945): 2.

Armstrong, Elisabeth. *Gender and Neoliberalism: The All-India Democratic Women's Association and Its Strategies of Resistance*. New Delhi: Leftword, 2020.

———. "Indian Peasant Women's Activism in a Hot Cold War." In *Communist Histories*, edited by Vijay Prashad, 1:176–217. New Delhi: Leftword Books, 2016.

Bandyopadhyay, Gita. *Ek Dub Dui Dub (One Dip, Two Dips)*. Kolkata: Kabi Pokkho, 1998.

Bhattacharya, Malini, and Abhijit Sen, eds. *Talking of Power: Early Writings of Bengali Women from the Mid 19th Century to the Beginning of the 20th Century*. Kolkata: Stree, 2003.

Chakravartty, Gargi. "Emergence of Mahila Atma Raksha Samiti in the Forties—Calcutta Chapter." In *The Stormy Decades: Calcutta*, edited by Tanika Sarkar and Sekhar Bandyopadhyay, 177–203. New Delhi: Social Science Press, 2015.

Chattopadhyay, Suchetana. *An Early Communist: Muzaffar Ahmad in Calcutta 1913–1929*. New Delhi: Tulika Books, 2011.

Cooper, Adrienne. *Sharecropping and Sharecroppers' Struggles in Bengal, 1930–1950*. Kolkata: K.P. Bagchi, 1988.

Cumings, Bruce. *The Origins of the Korean War*. Vols. 1 and 2. Princeton, NJ: Princeton University Press, 1981.

Custers, Peter. *Women in the Tebhaga Uprising: Rural Poor Women and Revolutionary Leadership (1946–47)*. Kolkata: Naya Prokash, 1987

Dutt, R. Palme. *Fascism and Social Revolution*. San Francisco: Proletarian Publisher, 1934.

Forbes, Geraldine. *Women in Modern India*. Cambridge, UK: Cambridge University Press, 1988.

Frazier, Jessica. *Women's Antiwar Diplomacy During the Vietnam War Era*. Chapel Hill: University of North Carolina Press, 2017.

Hong, Young-Sun. *Cold War Germany, the Third World, and the Global Humanitarian Regime*. New York: Cambridge University Press, 2015.

Hore, Bratati. "Role Played by the Peasant Women in the Tebhaga Movement: Problem of Political Theorization." *Proceedings of the Indian History Congress* 50 (1989): 547–53.

Jalil, Rakhshanda. *A Rebel and Her Cause: The Life and Work of Rashid Jahan*. New Delhi: Women Unlimited, 2014.

Jones, Claudia. "International Women's Day and the Struggle for Peace." *Political Affairs* 29, no. 3 (1950): 32–45.

———. "Speech to the Court, February, 1953" *Thirteen Communists Speak in Court*, 121–23. New York: New Century Publications, 1953.

Khan, Yasmine. *The Raj at War: A People's History of India's Second World War*. Gurgaon, Haryana: Random House India, 2015.

———. "Sex in an Imperial War Zone: Transnational Encounters in Second World War India." *History Workshop Journal* 73, no. 1 (2012): 240–58.

Kumar, Radha. *The History of Doing: An Illustrated Account of Movements for Women's Rights and Feminism in India, 1800–1990*. New York: Verso, 1993.

Kwan, Heonik. *After the Korean War*. Cambridge, UK: Cambridge University Press, 2020.

Lahiri, Abani. *Postwar Revolt of the Rural Poor in Bengal: Memoirs of a Communist Activist*. Kolkata: Seagull Books, 2001.

Leow, Rachel. "A Missing Peace: The Asia-Pacific Peace Conference in Beijing, 1952 and the Emotional Making of Third World Internationalism." In *The Lives of Cold War Afro-Asianism*, edited by Su Lin Lewis and Carolien Stolte. Leiden: University of Leiden Press, 2022.

Lewis, Su Lin. "Asian Socialism and the Forgotten Architects of Post-Colonial Freedom, 1952–1956." In *The Lives of Cold War Afro-Asianism*, edited by Su Lin Lewis and Carolien Stolte. Leiden: University of Leiden Press, 2022.

Liu, Zifeng. "Decolonialization is not a Dinner Party: Claudia Jones, China's Nuclear Weapons, and Anti-Imperialist Solidarity." *The Journal of Intersectionality* 3, no. 1 (Summer, 2019): 21–45.

Loomba, Ania. *Revolutionary Desires: Women, Communism, and Feminism in India*. New York: Routledge, 2019.

Majumdar, Asok. *The Tebhaga Movement: Politics of Peasant Protest in Bengal, 1946–1950*. New Delhi: Aakhar, 2011.

Marik, Soma. "Breaking Through a Double Invisibility: The Communist Women of Bengal, 1939–1948." *Critical Asian Studies*. 45, no. 1 (2013): 79–118.

Menon, Parvathi. *Breaking Barriers: Stories of Twelve Women*. New Delhi: Leftword Books, 2005.

Millard, Betty. "A Look at 'Operation Killer.'" *Masses and Mainstream* 4, no. 11 (November 1951): 15–22.

Morris-Suzuki, Teresa, ed. *The Korean War in Asia: A Hidden History*. Lanham, MD: Rowman & Littlefield, 2018.

Mukerjee, Madhusree. *Churchill's Secret War: The British Empire and the Ravaging of India during World War II*. Chennai: Tranquebar, 2010.

Mukherjee, Kanak. "Our Famine-Homeless Sisters' Plight: Bengal Government's Work Houses Closing Down." *People's War*, September 1944, 9.

Munro, John. *The Anticolonial Front: The African American Freedom Struggle and Global Decolonization, 1945–1960*. Cambridge, UK: Cambridge University Press, 2017.

Namboodiripad, E. M. S. *A History of Indian Freedom Struggle*. Trivandrum, Kerala: Social Scientist Press, 1986.

———. *Economics and Politics of India's Socialist Pattern*. New Delhi: People's Publishing House, 1966.

Panjabi, Kavita. *Unclaimed Harvest: An Oral History of the Tebhaga Women's Movement*. New Delhi: Zubaan, 2017.

Sarkar, Sumit, and Tanika Sarkar. *Women and Social Reform in Modern India: A Reader*. Bloomington: Indiana University Press, 2008.

"Second World Peace Congress, Warsaw, November 16–22, 1950." Supplement to *Voks Bulletin*, No. 66 (1951).

Sen, Samita. "Honor and Resistance: Gender, Community and Class in Bengal, 1920–40." In *Bengal: Communities, Development and States*, edited by Sekhar Bandyopadhyay, Ahijit Dasgupta, and Willem can Schendel, 209–54. Delhi: Manohar, 1994.

Sen, Sunil. *The Working Women and Popular Movements in Bengal: from the Gandhi Era to the Present Day*. Kolkata: K.P. Bagchi & Co, 1985.

Shen, Zhihua. *Mao, Stalin and the Korean War: Trilateral Communist Relations in the 1950s*. New York: Routledge, 2012.

Strong, Anna Louise. *In North Korea: First Eye-Witness Report*. New York: Soviet Russia Today, 1949.

Swedlow, Amy. *Women Strike For Peace: Traditional Motherhood and Radical Politics in the 1960s*. Chicago: University of Chicago Press, 1993.

Thapar-Bjorkert, Suruchi. *Women in the National Movement: Unseen Faces, Unheard Voices, 1930–42*. New Delhi: Sage, 2006.

Wittner, Lawrence S. *One World or None: A History of the World Nuclear Disarmament Movement Through 1953*. Vol. 1, *The Struggle Against the Bomb*. Stanford, CA: Stanford University Press, 1993.

Conclusion

Khan, Nighat Said. "Up Against the State: The Women's Movement in Pakistan and Its Implications for the Global Women's Movement." In *Politics, Activism and Vision: Local and Global Challenges*, edited by Luciana Ricciutelli, Angela Miles, and Margaret H. McFadden, 79–96. London: Zed Books, 2004.

Wiley-Yancy, Destiny. "Afro-Asian Peoples' Solidarity Organization (AAPSO) Presidium Committee Nairobi Preparations." *Meridians* 20, no. 1 (April 2021): 174–82.

INDEX

Abidjan Women's Committee, 6, 147
ACDWF (All China Democratic Women's Federation), 2, 35, 81, 84–85, 105–6
adivasi, 123
African Democratic Assembly, RDA (Reassemblement Democratique Africain), 1–2, 4
agricultural workers, 3, 8, 123. *See also* peasant women; rural women
All China Democratic Women's Federation. *See* ACDWF
All-India Students Federation of India, 115
Allouchiche, Baya, 51, 70, 109–10
Andreen, Andrea, 11, 61, 91
anti-colonial feminism, 18–21, 56, 89–90, 97–100, 110, 148–51. *See also* internationalist left feminism; socialist feminism
anti-colonialism, 5–6, 8, 12–13, 18–21, 28–30, 111–13, 150–51. *See also* anti-colonial movements

anti-colonial movements, 5–6, 8, 42–44, 88, 97–98, 112–13, 118–21, 130, 150–51
anti-communism, 15–16, 51, 91, 139–45
anti-fascism, 3, 18, 28–30, 46, 63–64, 69, 130
anti-imperialism: anti-imperialist struggles, 38, 92, 148; internationalism, 15, 17–22, 93, 130; women's movement, 8, 34, 52, 83, 112–13, 148–50; women's political strategy, 2–3, 46
anti-racism, 18
anti-Semitism, 63–64
Asian Relations Conference, 34, 36
Asian Women's Conference. *See* AWC
Asian Women's Conference in Tokyo, 81–82
Associated Negro Press, 51
Averink, Hanna, 63–64
AWC (Asian Women's Conference): aspirations, 7–8, 49–55,

AWC *(continued)*
  60, 82–83; conjunctural analysis, 109–13; description, 7, 14, 84–100; participants, 1–2, 7, 7–13, 79–80; praxis developed, 7–14, 17–18, 20–22, 104, 146–48; preparations for, 122–24, 127, 132, 146–49

Bandung conference, 2
Bandyopadhyay, Gita, 9, 15, 114–36, *133*, 139–45, *144*
Bass, Charlotta, 81
Begum, Hajrah, 34, 153
Bengal famine, 25–26, 43, 124
Bertrand, Simone, 50, 125
Bose, Taruna, 100
Boummi, Salma, 66, 139
Broussan, Adeline, 126
Buchaca, Edith, 47, 129, 138
Bulletin Anglais, 133. See also *Information Bulletin*

Cai, Chang, 15, 39–44, 46, 85, 104–5
Campbell, Arturo, 72
capitalism, 19, 21, 42, 46, 60, 99, 101–2, 116–21, 124, 131, 147
Chakravartty, Gargi, 140–41
Chakravartty, Renu, 25–26
Chase, Michelle, 129, 138–39
Chen Bo'er, 84–85
Chen, Xiu Zhu, 103
Chhatri Sangh, 114–15
Clayton Plan, 47–49
Cold War, 15, 98
colonialism, 3, 5–7, 16, 18, 21, 30–34, 42–43, 50, 62, 65, 75, 88, 102, 110, 116–21, 146
communism, 23–24, 32, 54–55, 62, 69, 97, 116, 142–43
Communist Party of China, 80, 84, 107, 122
Communist Party of Cuba, 47

Communist Party of India. *See* CPI
Communist Party of Indonesia (PKI), 76, 93
Communist Party of Malaya, 103–4
Communist Party of the United States of America. *See* CPUSA
Communist Party of Venezuela, 47
communist women's movement, 10, 15, 32, 36
Congress of American Women, 51, 90–91
Congress Party of India, 36, 122–24
Congress Party for the Independence of Madagascar, 15, 65
conjunctural analysis, 21–22, 38–44, 93, 109
Cotton, Eugenie, 28, 125–26
Coulibaly, Celestine Ouezzin, 1, 3–8, 15–16, 51, 147–48
CPI (Communist Party of India), 114, 121–22, 140–41
CPUSA (Communist Party of the United States of America), 9, 51, 139–40
Cumings, Bruce, 128

Daily Worker, 67
Dale, Thelma, 27, 30–31
Dalit (oppressed caste) women, 27, 123. *See also* non-caste Hindus
"Daughters of China," 84–85
De Beurijding (The Liberator), 67
De Haan, Francisca, 15
Deng, Yingchao, 104–7
Devi, Katyayani, 114
Ding, Ling, 65–66
Dulles, John Foster, 53
Dulmavshav, Jsivigruydin, 71
Duong The Hauh, 27–29

Edelman, Fanny, 48–49

Faroqi, Mahine, 66, 100
fascism, 16, 24, 28, 30, 64, 88, 130–31
feminist anti-colonialism, 55, 88
feminist internationalism: as a praxis, 9, 12–13; two visions for, 98
feudalism, 27, 34
Firouz, Maryam, 66
Founding Conference of the Women's International Democratic Federation, Paris, 1945, 10, 17, 22, 26–32
French Communist Party, 96, 126

Ganguly, Pratibha, 124–25, 142–43
Global South, 18, 149
Guomindang, 47, 107

Handoo, Jaikishore, 28, 32–33
"Hands Off Korea" campaign, 135–40
Hasan, Amine Araf, 66, 139
Hatta government, 75–77
Helou, Victoria, 66
Hodinova, Anezka, 70
Hookham, Kutty, 45
Ho Thi Minh, 59–60, 78–80, 82, 83, 86–87, 95
House on Un-American Activities Commission. *See* HUAC
HUAC (House on Un-American Activities Commission), 91
Hukbalahap Rebellion, Philippines, 81

imperialism, 2, 17, 20, 28, 32, 40, 46–49, 71, 74, 91, 146
Information Bulletin, 10, 13, 36, 92–93, 126

inside/outside: contradiction, 29–30; political praxis, 12, 27, 149; solidarity, 2–3, 30–31, 55
International Women's Day, 92, 139–40
internationalism: definition, 145; praxis, 94; socialist internationalism, 129, 140; solidarity, 129; women's, 11–12, 27, 83, 85, 97
internationalist left feminism, 11–12, 18–19, 56–57. *See also* socialist feminism
International Union of Students. *See* IUS
IUS (International Union of Students), 38, 74

Jackson, Ada, 72, 90
Japanese Democratic Women's Council, 81–82
Jones, Claudia, 139–40

Khan, Nighat Said, 149–50
Khanum, Tamara, 71
Kim, Suzy, 98, 108, 129
Kim, Taewoo, 55, 138
Korean War: international peace movement, 135–40, 145; "Save Our Sons" campaign, 14, 139; US-led war, 17, 52–55, 89, 91, 107–9; WIDF, 42, 127–29, 136; World Peace Council, 127–29
Kowani, 60
Kurtosudirdjo, 67

left feminism, 15, 110–11
Lenin, V. I, 41, 46
Ling, Lang, 80, 83
Liu, Shaoqi, 96–97
Lu, Cui, 34–37, 35, 46–47, 50, 122, 125
Luzardo, Olga, 47

Madiun Affair, 76
Mahila Atmaraksha Samiti or Women's Self-Defense League. *See* MARS
Malagasy Solidarity Committee, 65
MARS (*Mahila Atmaraksha Samiti* or Women's Self-Defense League), 24–26, 115, 123–25
Marshall Plan, 47–49
Marxism, 8, 15, 22–23, 32, 42, 54, 101–2, 116–18; *See also* Marxist-Leninism
Marxist feminism, 8, 15
Marxist-Leninism, 8
Mason, Vivian Carter, 33
masses: movement, 2, 8, 22–24, 123–24; organization, 16, 23–24, 27–28; protest, 12–14, 30, 124–25
McCarren Act, 139
Merens, Jeanne, 31–33
Millard, Betty, 9, 70–77, 90, 126, 129–30, 138–39
Milosevic, Olga, 72–73, 90
Mire, Koikari, 81–82
Miyamoto, Yuriko, 81
motherhood, 89–92, 98, 102–4, 131; *See also* revolutionary motherhood
Mothers Conference, Lausanne, 1955, 10
Mukhyopadhyay, Subhas, 144
Munsi, Vidya, 28

National Council for American-Soviet Friendship
national independence, 4, 24, 34, 39–40, 44, 50, 67, 74, 76–77, 79–80, 83, 94, 107, 112–13
national liberation, 40, 43–44, 82, 96
National Liberation Front. *See* NLF

national self-determination, 31, 86, 88, 89, 97
National Negro Congress, 27
New Masses, 126
New World Review, 51
NLF (National Liberation Front), 78
non-caste Hindus, 56
non-governmental feminist organizations, 149
non-profit industrial complex, 149

Odinot-Lips, Rie (Marie), 63–64, 93–94

Pak, Chŏng-ae, 107–9, 136
Parfanova, Naidezhda, 72–73, 90, 99
Patnaik, Prabhat, 59
Patnaik, Utsa, 59
patriarchy, 3, 6, 16, 27, 86, 88, 141, 147
Pauker, Ana, 33
peace, 8, 21, 44–45, 53, 61, 82, 83, 92, 95, 98, 100, 127–28, 140
peasant women, 23, 43, 56–58, 98, 121, 123, 140–41. *See also* agricultural workers; rural women
Perhimpunan Indonesia. *See* PI
Pham, Ngoc Thuan, 49–50, 80
PI (Perhimpunan Indonesia), 63–64, 67
polygamy, 147
praxis, 9, 12, 14, 17–19, 55, 58, 84, 88–93, 99–100, 140, 146–47
primitive accumulation, 125–27
propaganda, 10–14, 52–58, 112
pro-socialism, 8, 12, 39, 50, 102–3, 129, 150

Rabesahala, Gisele, 15, 51, 65, 110, 112
racism, 16, 30–32, 45, 55, 77, 88

Ramelson, Marion, 11, 94
Ransome-Kuti, Funmilayo, 50–51
Ravensbruck, 63
Red Army, 31
Reid, Ela, 26–30
Renville Agreement, 76
reproductive labor, 19, 100–104
revolutionary feminism, 19, 88, 90, 121–25
revolutionary motherhood, 12, 19–20, 98, 100–104, 127, 131
Rhee, Syngman, 107–9, 128
Ricardo, David, 48
Robeson, Eslanda (Essie), 51–53, 72, 90
Robeson, Paul, 51, 72
Rodriguez, Candelaria, 129, 138
rural women, 5, 23, 57, 98, 109, 112–13, 145. *See also* agricultural workers; peasant women

Second International Congress of Women, 1948, Budapest, 10, 14, 37–49, 61, 66, 80, 90–92, 104, 125, 130–32, 136
Sen, Manikuntala, 25
Smith Act (the Alien Registration Act), 139
Smith, Adam, 120
social boycott, 142
socialism, 16, 19, 32, 45, 52, 82, 85, 88, 117, 129, 145
socialist feminism, 56, 149
Soesilo, Brenthel, 62, 69, 71–72
Soesilo, Nyonya, 62
Soesilo, Raden, 62, 69
solidarity, 2–3, 12, 15, 18–20, 30, 33, 42, 77, 112–13. *See also* anti-colonialism; internationalist left feminism; Korean War
solidarity of complicity, 110
Song, Qingling, 81–82

Songgram government, 81
Sportisse, Alice, 31
Suripno, 67, 74–76
Suripno, Lillah (Soesilo), 60–77, *68*, 93–94

Tanaga, Hamaku, 81
"Tangkuban Prahoe" ("The Upturned Boat"), 68, *68*
Tebhaga movement, 57, 123, 140–41
Third International Congress of Women, 1953, Copenhagen, 10, 14, 144–45, 153
Third World, 56, 100, 150
Ting, Thien Gui, 80–81, 83
transnational feminism, 15, 56, 149
Transvaal Women's Union of South Africa, 45
Truman Plan, 49
Tudeh Party, 66

Union of French Women, 94–96
Union of Vietnamese Women, 82
Union of Women of Abeokuta, 32
United Nations, 33, 52–53, 75, 132, 138, 149
United Nations Conference on Women, Nairobi, 1985, 148–49

Vaillant-Couturier, Marie Claude, 33, *35, 105*
Vermeersch, Jeannette, 47, 70–77, 95–66, *95*
Vietnamese Women's Union of Paris, 27
Vietnam War, 78–80, 82, 86–87, 89, 95–96, 110
Vught, 69

Wang, Zheng, 106
We Accuse!, 14, 136–38

WFDY (World Federation of Democratic Youth and Students), 28, 36, 38, 45, 74, 106, 121–22
WFTU (World Federation of Trade Unions), 38
WIDF (Women's International Democratic Federation), 2, 8–14, 17–21, 26–56, 60–61, 102–4, 115, 121–22, 126, 130–32, 148. *See also* Asian Women's Conference; "Hands Off Korea" campaign; Second International Congress of Women, 1948, Budapest; Third International Congress of Women, 1953, Copenhagen
Women of the Whole World, 13
Women's Anti-Fascist conference, 24
Women's Anti-Fascist League, 37
Women's Bureau, Afro-Asian People's Solidarity Organization (AAPSO), 148–49
women's emancipation, 83, 88, 142–43

women's equality, 87, 112–13, 129
Women's International Democratic Federation. *See* WIDF
women's rights, 8, 21, 82–83, 88–89, 96–97, 100, 110–11, 141
working-class women, 23, 27, 43, 73, 101–2
World Federation of Democratic Youth and Students. *See* WFDY
World Federation of Trade Unions. *See* WFTU
World Peace Council. *See* WPC
World socialist movement, 40–41
World War II, 16, 17, 18, 21, 24–30, 39–40, 42, 97, 115–17, 120, 149
WPC (World Peace Council), 125, 127

Young Communist League, 99
Yu, Xixuan, 84

Zele, Rasoanoro, 112
Zhdanov, Andrei, 41
Zhou Enlai, 71, 84, 105–6

Founded in 1893,
UNIVERSITY OF CALIFORNIA PRESS
publishes bold, progressive books and journals
on topics in the arts, humanities, social sciences,
and natural sciences—with a focus on social
justice issues—that inspire thought and action
among readers worldwide.

The UC PRESS FOUNDATION
raises funds to uphold the press's vital role
as an independent, nonprofit publisher, and
receives philanthropic support from a wide
range of individuals and institutions—and from
committed readers like you. To learn more, visit
ucpress.edu/supportus.

www.ingramcontent.com/pod-product-compliance
Lightning Source LLC
Chambersburg PA
CBHW031437160426
43195CB00010BB/765